Reviewer's

The author skillfully draws us into the lives of the characters and through their lives we are sensitized to the destructive effects of war. ***The Promise***, in essence, helps us personalize war and thus we gain some understanding of the long reaching effects of this most tragic cataclysm upon all mankind and it s children.

Don McKay - Black Hat Publishing

Having grown up post WWII, and not being a fan of war movies or books, I was pretty much ignorant of the realities of WWI. Your book changed all that,

Iris Tuftin - author of *Cowboy Up Cole*

Set at the time of the First World War. Eric Brown's historical novel, ***The Promise***, transported us from Toronto, Canada, to England to war-torn France. It is story of love and adventure, loyalty, fast friendship, independence and it gives the reader an insight into British Class Distinction of the time.

Brown describes the horror and the reality of war, taking us inside the trenches where we've never before visited.

For those of you who enjoyed ***Ginny***. You will appreciate hearing her brother Paul's story.

Lillian Ross - Grassroots Publishing

THE

PROMISE

ERIC J BROWN

Brown Eric J (Eric John) 1947 –
  The Promise

ISBN 0-9684384-4-X

  Historic-Canadian-Fiction. 1. Title

PS8553.R68497P762004   C813'.54

C2004-903568-1

Printed and Published by
Magnolia Press
Box 499
Entwistle, Alberta
T0E 0S0

Dedication

This work is dedicated, firstly to the memory of all those who gave their lives to the illusive cause of patriotism. Secondly, this work is dedicated to all peace loving citizens of planet Earth as a reminder that the horror of war should never be an option for settling differences between nations.

Other Books Written by Eric J Brown
Ginny – A Canadian Story of Love & Friendship
1998
Ingrid – An Immigrant's Tale 2000
Anna – Her Odyssey to Freedom 2002
To the Last Tree Standing 2006
Third Time Lucky 2009

First Edition June 2004

Second Printing April 2006

Copyright 2004 © Eric J Brown

Acknowledgments

Producing a novel is not the work of one person alone but a team effort, with that I would like to thank the following people for taking the time to read and critique this work:

Firstly, Vi Stirling, for her overview of this work.
Secondly, Don & Barb McKay, for their detailed editing.
Thirdly, Lillian Ross and Iris Tuftin for their thorough final edit.

The scrutiny and suggestions offered by all of these people were vital to the success of this work.

I would also like to thank my good wife Isabella for her patience during the many long hours spent developing this work and her own suggestions concerning the outlay of this work

Finally, I would also like to give acknowledgment to, Erich Maria Remarque, whose classic novel, *All Quiet on the Western Front* helped serve as an inspiration for this work. This searing portrayal of the horrors of war through the eyes of a German soldier, gave much insight into the true folly of the Great War.

Author's Note

While I have striven to keep the main events surrounding the Battle of the Somme as historically accurate as possible, I have taken a few liberties for the sake of colouration.

For example, there is no evidence that a Scottish piper played a sad lament over his fallen comrades on that dreadful opening day of the Somme offensive. However, upon hearing the moving strains of *Hector the Hero* being played on the pipes, it seemed so appropriate for the scene. That these strains should touch the hearts of the German soldiers opposing them also is not out of line with the curious humanity that solders of the opposing armies showed one another when not engaged in killing each other. Soldiers often took time out to treat the wounded from the other side even in the heat of battle and there were even reports of German soldiers stealing over to the British lines at night to beg cigarettes which the tommies would give to them. Unlike the Second World War there was no opposing ideologies or mad dictators instigating conflict, no forces of good and evil, only blundering kings and politicians who foolishly allowed this carnage to unfold.

Also I took the liberty to have some Canadian soldiers temporarily assigned to a British unit so that the hero of the story could have eyewitness to the foolish suicide attack on the German lines by the British during that catastrophic opening day of the battle. Such temporary assignment is feasible, as at that time the Canadian Army was still considered part of the greater British Army and its senior commanders were British generals.

Foreword

For those of you who read my first novel, *Ginny - A Canadian Story of Love and Friendship,* you may recall she had a brother named Paul, whom she idolized, as having been killed in the Great War during the Battle of the Somme. Almost from the time that *Ginny* was released, I have always wanted to write his story. While his fate had been predetermined even before the plot was laid out, I chose to carry on for three reasons.

<u>One</u>. I've always been a history buff particularly of modern history, with a fascination for progression of the two so-called world wars. With this in mind, I've always wanted to write a war story involving Canadian soldiers.

<u>Two</u>. I could have chosen a more positive theme such as the heroic stand at Ypres in the face of poison gas, the incredible endurance of our boys at the giant mud bog of Passchendaele or the crowning victory at Vimy Ridge, which defined the Canadian Army as one of the worlds great armies. Instead I chose the epic Battle of the Somme, one of the darkest features of the war, where hundreds of thousands of young men from all over the British Empire were foolishly sacrificed in relentless human wave/suicide attacks on the German trenches. This, all because the senior British commanders were determined to batter their way through the German lines at any cost. I did this because, in spite of my fascination with the wars, I am anti war in spirit and what better venue could I choose to display the folly of war, than a story that involves the Battle of the Somme.

<u>Three</u>. The combination of wanting to write a story about Ginny's brother and to deliver a stinging rebuttal to war, gave me a flash of insight. I could write a novel with both plenty of battlefield action and deliver a very

powerful anti war message, simply because I had the unwitting foresight to have him involved in the Battle of the Somme in my original work.

As for those who think they know how this work will end even before they read it, I have hopefully, injected enough undercurrent and mystery into this work so that none will know exactly how or why it ended as it did without reading it first.

For all of you who enjoyed the heartwarming saga of *Ginny - A Canadian Story of Love & Friendship,* this work will offer some vignettes of Ginny at an earlier age. It will also offer insight into the underlying reasons other than the love of Marty, which caused Ginny to readily abandon her sheltered life for the rigorous one of a homesteaders' wife.

Chapter One
October 1916

The autumn sunset was red as it broke through the skies. It offered the first hopeful relief from the torrential rains that had inundated them these past weeks, turning their world into a sticky ooze and their trench into a drainage ditch. The sky was red to the southwest behind them, red like the churned up earth of the no-man's-land ahead of them between that of their barbed wire and that of the Hun. Red was the ground from the blood of two mighty armies locked perpetually in combat in a battle that was seemingly without resolution. The ground was red, the trenches were red. Everything was red; red with the blood from the flower of youth from both the Grand Empire and the German Reich.

The awful whine of an incoming artillery shell could be heard and Paul hunkered down, hunching his shoulders like a turtle trying to draw its head into its shell. The shell exploded a few yards away and Paul was showered with great clogs of mud and a few chunks of wood and metal that bounced off his helmet. Its soup plate-like design was ideal for deflecting this incessant rain of debris from exploding shells.

"Do you think the Hun is getting ready to come over the top at us, Curtis,?" Paul asked his buddy who stood beside him in the trench. Curtis was not only Paul's buddy, but also his sergeant. Since Paul had risen to corporal at the same time as Curtis rose to squad commander, they were able to maintain their close friendship without a serious breach of rank protocol.

"Hard to say," Curtis shrugged. "They lost so many men, it's a wonder they have enough left to come at us again."

"They always find more, just like we always find more," Paul said dryly. He tilted his helmet back slightly and wiped the sweat and mud spray off his forehead.. Though Paul was considered a handsome man with his wavy brown hair and youthful features with his bright innocent-looking eyes, some of the allure of his looks were beginning to wear off from the continuous horror show he found himself in, since the first of July. It would still be a little over two months until he reached his twentieth birthday, but he both felt and looked several years older.

"They'll probably want back the land we took from them these past months," Curtis said with a weak laugh. Curtis at twenty-three was taller and more rugged looking than his friend. His blunt determined chin projecting the ability to take command of a given situation had caught the eye of his superiors. This and the enormous casualty rate inflicted on their regiment had allowed him to quickly rise to the rank of staff sergeant and squad commander.

"Yeah," Paul said with disdain. "In four months we've advanced four miles. How many months will it take to reach Berlin?"

"Never mind Berlin, we'll be old and gray before we even reach Belgium," Curtis added. Then as he instinctively fumbled with the cigarette case in his tunic pocket he remembered, "Hey Paul, got a smoke? I'm out."

"Yeah, no problem," Paul replied as he reached inside the mud-caked tunic of his Khaki uniform for his metal cigarette case.

Another shell exploded a short distance away as Paul opened his cigarette case for Curtis. He observed two bodies leap upward from the explosion to land on the upturned earth. Butchery like this had long ceased to have any effect on Paul, he had seen so much of it. It only mattered that it was not his body or perhaps that of Curtis that went flying through the air. As Paul lit a smoke for himself, the Canadian artillery was beginning to return fire.

"Nah, I don't think the Hun will be coming over the top," Curtis remarked as he puffed on his cigarette. "We're shooting back."

"Maybe we'll be going over the top," Paul replied.

"They'll give us a grog and a sermon first though," Curtis added, exhaling.

"Maybe," was Paul's only comment as he stood against the forward side of the trench. "Sometimes they get a sudden urge to attack and over the top we go."

They watched the sunset fade into twilight while the new moon merely a slim crescent offered scant illumination before it too dropped below the horizon. The only other light being provided was by the unnatural lightning-like flashes of the artillery duels. In the trenches behind them, Paul could hear the slurping sounds of many feet waddling in the mud. It had rained so much recently that the duckboards placed at the bottoms of the main trenches had been pushed into the mud. They would have to be pried up and reset soon.

"Our relief is coming," Curtis commented.

"Yeah we can exchange this mud-hole for the one that is our quarters," Paul replied, as he shouldered his rifle.

"Well, the billet will be a relief from the past few nights we had to spend out here in the mud." Curtis commented.

"Yeah." Paul looked at the hollow in the side of the trench that offered scant shelter from the elements during their watch. Now another soldier would occupy it and perhaps even improve upon it.

The relief troops filed in among them and Curtis called for his squad to go to the rear. Little was said between the sets of soldiers changing places. Paul and Curtis merely slogged on through the muddy trenches of the maze that connected the front line trenches to those at the rear where their billets were located. As they went past dugouts containing cannons, Paul and Curtis put their hands over their ears never knowing when one of them might fire as an artillery duel was in progress.

The terrible whine of an incoming shell could be heard and Paul and the others leaned hard against the muddy bank of the trench. There was an unusually loud explosion as it struck nearby.

"It got one of our cannons," Curtis cried as they saw a still-spinning cannon wheel bounce over the top of the trench amid a shower of mud.

"Either we or the Hun will be going over the top soon," Paul said as they continued on their way. "The cannons always duel just before an attack by one side or the other."

They slogged their way to their billet, which consisted of a large wooden cribbed bunker dug into the ground. They deposited their gear then went on to the mess tent. As usual their meal consisted of beans, potatoes, and mutton. It was often all cooked together in one vat and doled out on their plates as one big glob. Tonight they got a treat of fresh biscuits.

"The beans and potatoes are standard," Paul said, grimacing as he chewed the tallowy meat, "but this endless ration of stewed mutton is getting pretty sickening."

"At least we get to eat back here this time," Curtis replied referring to the mess area. "The last while we had to eat in the trenches. At least this meal is hot. Our recent fare of bully beef was always cold."

"Yeah," Paul said as he pushed his now empty meal tray ahead. "It was nice of the cooks to make biscuits for a change. Now if they'd only learn to make pies."

"There are some MP poking around, asking questions," a soldier sitting across the table from them remarked.

"Oh what are they after?" Curtis asked carefully. He stole a glance at Paul noticing an uncomfortable look sweep across Paul's face at the mention of the military police.

"Dunno, nobody'll say. Probably somebody is in trouble, or something. It seems like they are interested in talking to the boys of C Company."

"Yeah," Paul swallowed. He was thinking of the incident with Lieutenant Bedford a while back. *'Did someone snitch?'*

Curtis smiled at Paul and lit a cigarette. "Probably someone went AWOL or something."

"Yeah," Paul replied quietly.

"Going AWOL is a good way to get shot," the other soldier remarked

Paul was about to rise from the table, as he found reference to the firing squad unsettling in light of the incident with Lieutenant Bedford. The soldier designated as courier came in and cried, "Mail call!"

Everyone's attention was rapt as letters and parcels from home were the mainstay that kept these soldiers going. When the mailman called out "Cunningham," Paul was handed two letters and a parcel.

"All from Toronto," he said in a low voice as he checked the return address on each envelope. He had a letter each from his mother and his sister Ginny. The parcel was from both of them.

"Nothing from the lady from Kent," Curtis said wryly, referring to Paul's sweetheart, Chelsea, in England. Curtis also received a letter and parcel from home.

"No," Paul sighed. It would be his fondest hope that he might receive a letter from Chelsea, but he knew that was a fools dream. Chelsea was busy entertaining royalty or singing in Paris. She no longer had time for a lonely Canadian soldier. Some of the soldiers tore into their mail on the spot. Paul, however, carried his mail back to his bunk to read it there.

As he and Curtis walked back to the billet, Curtis put an arm on his shoulder and said, "You seem a little worried buddy."

"I get nervous when there are MP around. Did you hear that other guy? They are interviewing soldiers from C

Company. That's us"

"Like I said before, if they were after you, you'd be in the stockade by now," Curtis assured him. "You worry too much. Most of the others present at the incident are either dead like the old sarge, or PoW like Bob."

"I just wished that incident hadn't happened," Paul said with a troubled voice.

"It couldn't be avoided. Bedford was obviously quite insane," Curtis assured him. "If they should ever haul you up before the tribunal we will all stand behind you."

"If only he hadn't been been killed."

"If he'd a lived you'd be in prison, or shot. Now, lets forget about it and enjoy your mail and parcel," Curtis said as they approached the billet.

Paul set the mail on his cot and unwound the mud clogged puttees from his legs, shook the dirt out of them, then removed his grimy boots. He took off his wet socks and carefully wiped his feet, then dusted them with a newly issued powder that was supposed to guard against trench foot, that horrible toe-destroying fungus that had crippled many a soldier. Keeping his feet as dry as possible was the best defense against the dreaded malady.

With his dirty outerwear off he could now relax on his bunk and learn the news from home. He opened his parcel.

"Socks, wonderful!" he exclaimed, holding up a pair of homemade knitted socks. It was one of three pair in his parcel. He quickly put on one pair, savouring the warmth on his still-damp feet.

"Got an extra pair for me?" Curtis laughed.

"Afraid not. Ginny made these socks."

"Ginny, your sister?" Curtis asked, somewhat surprised. "I thought she'd spend her time at tea parties and bridge tables. After all, isn't that what rich girls do?"

"Ginny doesn't consider herself a rich girl." Paul replied. "That is why we get along so well. She likes things like sewing and knitting." He laughed and continued, "Father is always at her for doing things with her hands, instead of honing her skills at bridge and social etiquette. Even Mom thinks that holding a tea cup properly is much more important than sewing." Then with a put-on face he added, "Sewing is a maid's job you know."

"Ginny, I take it, doesn't think much of being a lady?" Curtis chuckled.

"Ginny is a great lady," Paul reiterated. "She comes by it naturally without needing any training." Paul continued to expose the contents of his parcel.

The parcel also contained two large packages, one containing hard candy and the other peanuts, some small packages of exotic flavours of tea and coffee, hot chocolate powder, and two paperback novels by Paul's favourite author. Most importantly, the parcel contained three cartons of tailor-made cigarettes. Cigarettes were gold, not only were they a nerve-calming necessity to virtually every soldier, but they were the currency by which one could bargain with both fellow soldiers and French civilians.

"I'll give you twelve francs for two packages of smokes and an handful of candy," one of his comrades named Dale said.

"What would I do with twelve francs?" Paul laughed.

"Twelve francs will get you an overnight stay at Madam Reni's bordello next time we get leave in Ameins."

"If I want a whore, I'll bargain directly with the cigarettes," Paul replied. He thought of the small French city near the front that offered all manner of entertainment for the battle-weary troops. He then replied, "However, for five francs, I'll give you one package of cigarettes and a small handful of both candy and peanuts."

"It's a deal." Dale fished out a five-franc note and the exchange was made.

"I'll give you five pounds for a pair of socks," another soldier offered, knowing the British currency was much more valuable than the French money.

"The socks aren't for sale at any price," Paul replied, "and I'll kill anyone trying to steal them. If you need extra socks, get your loved ones back home to make you a pair." He tucked the other two pairs of socks under his bottom blanket below his pillow, as he knew a soldier would do just about anything to have dry socks. Another soldier came over to Paul's bunk holding a small package of cheap cigars. "Trade you for a pack of cigarettes," he said in a quiet voice. "They put cigars in my parcel and I hate cigars."

"Okay," Paul replied and the swap was made.

Paul lit one of the cigars, filling the billet with its powerful aroma. "Now if you don't mind I'd like to read my letters from home," he said as he laid back on his bunk with his letters in his hand and the rest of the parcel at his feet. Later he would have to put all food items in a metal container to avoid attracting rats. Some of the men of the squad continued to bargain with others over the contents of their parcels, but Paul was left alone to read his letters.

He quickly read the letter from his mother, all her letters were much the same. She missed him and worried about him. His letters from Ginny were always much more interesting, though they said much the same thing as his mother's letters. Ginny's letters were always better because Paul and his sister shared the secrets of their souls. He had told her all about Chelsea, but he dare not tell her of the incident with Lieutenant Bedford lest the censors read his mail.

As Paul listened to the dull pounding of the artillery exchange, scarcely different from so many he had heard before since he came to the front back in June, he again wondered how he had come to be in the midst of this man-made hell on earth. His mind wandered back to his childhood.

Paul Cunningham was born of a well-to-do Toronto family almost twenty years prior, before the last century had even ended. He did not remember when his first sister, Ginny, was born. It seemed that she was always there as a younger playmate and later confidant. He only knew that she had the distinction of being born on the first day of the twentieth century. He remembered that in the year that he started school another sister named Victoria was born, but she was just a little sister.

For as long as he could remember his father, Robert Cunningham, had lectured his children about their station in life. When he was ten years old, Paul's father took him on a tour of the assembly plant of the great Massey-Harris corporation where Robert worked in senior management in their legal department.

"Someday son," Robert said in his sermon-like tone," you may sit on the board of directors of this great company, or one like it. Canada is on the move as an industrial nation. Never set your sights any lower than that of a director or vice-president."

"Are you a director, Dad?" Paul asked.

"I am working toward it," Robert chuckled

"Are we rich?" Paul wondered.

"We are well off," Robert replied. "I worked very hard to get this far. I was fortunate to meet and win the love of your mother. She had connections."

"Are you saying, that when I am old enough, I should marry someone with connections?"

"Connections are important," Robert chuckled. "Of course, so is love, " he added as an afterthought.

"Do you love Mommy?"

"Of course I do," Robert said abruptly. "Come let me take you to the assembly area. I'll show you a machine that can tie knots in a string by itself."

"Tie knots?"

"Yes, a relatively new device called a grain binder." Robert chuckled. He was glad to divert his son's attention away from awkward personal questions that were beyond his years.

They went out of the assembly line part of the factory to an area where machinery was demonstrated for the distributors. They came up to a grain binder that had been set up for demonstration. It was all set up with its canvasses attached, and twine threaded into place, as if it were ready for the field. A small electrically driven treadmill was set up under the large cleated bull-wheel, which in the field, would supply power for the binder to operate. At Robert's request, the treadmill was switched on. Paul watched in fascination as the great mechanical monster came alive with all its multiple moving parts consisting of chains and sprockets, gears, a rapidly sliding cutting sickle and large rotating reel.

"Watch here," Robert said as he took Paul to one end of the binder where the twine was attached to the knotter. He nodded for the demonstrator to throw some straw on the cutting platform. Soon the canvassers conveyed the straw up and over to the end where a set of three rotating fingers packed it against the twine. This action activated a trip mechanism. Paul watched in awe as the needle came up drawing the string around the sheaf and through the knotter. The knot was mechanically tied and the twine cut. The sheaf then dropped off the edge of the machine.

"This machine will revolutionize agriculture," Robert said as if he were a class instructor. "A farmer can harvest a much larger crop than he could doing all the tying by hand. There is a great future in developing mechanized agriculture. A future that can be yours one day, Son."

This was the first of many outings on which Robert took Paul to, hopefully, instill in him the importance of rising high on the corporate ladder.

Chapter Two

Paul lay in his bunk reading his letter from Ginny while a flickering oil lamp shared with a comrade in the next bunk provided his only light. Ginny's letter began with her usual worried concern about his fate at the front. Then as he read about his sister's emerging social life, he chuckled.

> *Can you imagine, Father who has decreed that now that I am sixteen and half years old, I can be allowed out to date under certain strict guidelines and with suitably respectable young men of proper breeding. Since Father does not think me capable of selecting my own beaus, he arranged for my first date with a certain John Wilkinson, of the Wilkinson family. I agreed as this was to be my very first time out with a young gentleman, one who has his own automobile. A shiny new Oldsmobile, no less.*
>
> *While his automobile was impressive, I was less than impressed with his haughty, slightly effeminate manner. He got me off to a bad start by taking me to the opera, and you know how I hate opera. Perhaps if he had taken me to a play, a ballet or especially the symphony, things might have been better. It was the conversation on the way home however, that really put me off wanting anything more to do with him.*

As Paul read the letter with his sister's description of her very first date, he imagined the conversation.

"Did you enjoy the opera, Ginny?" John asked eagerly as they left the opera house. "The *Barber of Seville* is one of my favourites."

"It was all right," Ginny replied in a flat tone, as they walked along.

"I take it, that this was not one of your favourites?" John said with knitted brow.

"I'm afraid that opera isn't my preferred entertainment," Ginny replied mildly.

"What sort of entertainment do you like?"

"I like plays, I enjoy ballets and I really like listening to the symphony," Ginny replied.

"I don't like symphony," John declared. "Symphony is too German. Nearly all the composers such as Beethoven and Bach are either German or Austrian, and we are at war with these countries. I think it would be simply unpatriotic to go to a Beethoven concert or even a Wagner opera."

Irritated by his brash denunciation of her favourite entertainment, Ginny abruptly asked, "Have you joined up yet?"

"Are you quite insane?" he replied haughtily. "Me, go over and crawl around in some trench getting shot at."

"Our country is at war, you know," Ginny retorted.

"There are plenty of ways to help out the war effort besides joining the Army," John continued in a haughty tone. "I am involved in raising war bonds and helping our family raise money for medical supplies."

"That seems a job for women, older people, or those unable to join up," Ginny said. "My father wanted to get my brother a home-front job, but he joined up to fight for his country."

"Well, bully for him. I don't feel I should go. Let the sons of immigrants and the working class do the fighting to show appreciation for all that we offer them here in Canada."

"You sound like my father," Ginny said in a low voice.

"Your father is right you know. Your brother is foolish."

"At least my brother wasn't too good to go fight for King

and country, but you seem to be." Ginny retorted. She was becoming decidedly annoyed at the insolence of her escort.

When they reached his automobile, John attempted to help her in, but Ginny, to show her growing vexation quickly climbed in on her own.

"Why are you so obsessed with everyone having to join up because your brother did?" John continued as he went around to the driver's side to set the throttle controls.

"My brother has courage and a sense of duty."

John went around to the front and gave the motor a rapid crank. It fired almost immediately. As he withdrew the crank, the motor chugged and sputtered on its own.

"Let's not get carried away and allow foolish arguments to destroy our relationship," John said mildly as he climbed into the chugging automobile. He was quite taken by Ginny's great beauty and warmth prior to their sudden disagreement "Shall we stop at a coffee house before taking you home?"

"No thank you. I feel I should go straight home," Ginny said coldly.

"I am sorry if I offended you," John said in pleading voice as he put the car in gear. "I would like the pleasure of your company a while longer."

"If you are a gentleman, sir," Ginny said in an frigid tone,"you will take me home immediately."

"As you wish," he sighed. The remainder of their trip home was in relative silence. A few clumsy attempts at conversation by John drew only a clipped response from Ginny when she even bothered to reply at all.

When they reached the Cunningham residence, Ginny stepped from the car as soon as it stopped in the driveway. John quickly came around to try to escort her to the door, but Ginny icily told him, "I am quite capable of finding my own way."

"Would I be able to call on you again, Ginny," John asked

in a desperate tone. Despite her obvious hostility, he was loathe to let this beautiful young lady out of his life.

"I don't think so," Ginny said flatly. "I am only interested in young men who have courage to fight for our King and country. The next young man who calls on me must be wearing a uniform."

Ginny turned and quickly entered the house without further comment, while John stood outside for a long moment with a perplexed look on his face wondering what had gone wrong.

"Home early are you not?" Robert said as Ginny came into the parlour.

"Humpf," Ginny replied.

"Did you not have a good time with young John tonight?" Claire said mildly with a smile.

"No," Ginny replied flatly. "He took me to an opera, and I hate operas"

"He will be calling again will he not?" Robert asked hopefully.

"He may call but I won't answer. He insulted my brother and I don't want to see him again."

"What did he say?" Claire asked.

"He said Paul was a fool for joining up," and then with a put on voice she added, "he would never join up."

Robert's eyes rolled upward as he had similar thoughts regarding his son's decision. Then he asked, "You *are* going to see him again?"

"I don't think so," Ginny replied. "He is a self-centred bore. I was finding him increasingly irritating even before he insulted Paul's name."

"Do you know who he is?" Robert said, his voice rising. "He is part of a family that owns the biggest department store chain in Canada. Do you know what vistas could open up for you if you were to become his beau?"

"I am not interested in how much money he has or who

he is," Ginny replied in a sharp tone. "My beau will have to be someone special."

Robert groped for a reply and finally said, "You don't understand, he has connections."

"Is that what you raised me for, Father?" Ginny said brusquely. "Chattel to advance your connections?"

"I take exception to that remark," Robert retorted.

"Perhaps you should let Ginny choose her own beaus," Claire added quietly, though she was chuckling inwardly at the tirade.

"How could she throw this opportunity away? She'd be set for life." Then to Ginny, he said, "I think you should sleep on it and if he calls another time, give him another chance."

"Ha, I told him that he need not bother unless he was wearing a uniform and I mean it."

"You told him that?" Robert shouted.

"Yes, and if he calls, I will hide in my bedroom until he goes, and the same goes for any other person of your society that you try to slough off on me. Whoever I choose to be my beau will be my choice, not yours!" Ginny said adamantly.

"You're getting pretty cheeky are you not? Perhaps you are not ready yet to have any beaus."

"That would suit me," Ginny replied. "I would rather stay home than be forced to keep the company of some snob who thinks he is too good to fight for our country. Now if you will excuse me I would like to retire for the evening." Ginny turned and went upstairs. Robert called after her but to no avail."

"The nerve of that girl," Robert muttered. "How dare she challenge me like that."

"Well dear," Claire sighed. "You brought it upon yourself."

"Now, don't you go getting on at me," Robert scolded.

"I would not push Ginny if I were you," Claire continued. "She is a very strong-willed person, just like your son."

"At least women can't join the Army," Robert grumbled.

"No, but she can run away when she's older. She could, if pushed hard enough, marry some common labourer or farmer just to spite you."

"She wouldn't, would she?" Robert was now concerned.

"Just let her choose her own beaus in her own way." Claire smiled quietly. "I am sure she appreciates her station in life. Finishing school will instill that into her."

"I hope so dear, I hope so," Robert sighed.

*　　*　　*

An unusually loud explosion from a shell landing nearby rattled the billet. Dust to fell through the roof boards bringing Paul out of his letter as he cursed and shook the dust off his blanket.

"You enjoy your sister's letters don't you," Curtis observed.

"Listen to this from the sister of the rich kid," Paul replied as he began reading aloud a passage from Ginny's letter dealing with her rejection of a young man because he would not join the Army.

Some of the others laughed at the comment and Curtis said, "Good for her, Rich Kid. It's good to see a patriotic rich kid." Rich Kid had been Paul's nickname in training, and only his closest comrades were allowed to use it..

"I bet a rich kid like you must wonder at times what you are doing in the middle of this man-made hell, eh?" Dale added.

"Our country was at war, so I did what every patriotic young man would do," Paul replied blandly.

"Most of you guys from the upper class get a cushy job away from the front," Dale continued.

"I'm not upper class," Paul retorted. "Although my father would like to be."

"He ran away to join the army to spite his father," Curtis added.

"So that's it," Dale laughed. "You come down to get slaughtered like the rest of the plebes."

"I plan to survive this war," Paul said adamantly. "I made that promise to my sister from whom you have just heard."

"Sounds like you and your sister are real close," Dale said. "I'd like to meet her sometime. But then I wouldn't fit in with a rich kid."

"You'd laugh if you really knew how Ginny feels about being a so-called rich kid," Paul said, as he continued reading her letter.

Paul smiled as he thought of his sister. He thought back to the times when he and Ginny would share secret smirks as they listened to their father's many lectures about their station in life. He recalled one time when his father came home from work and found Ginny curled up in a chair in the parlour reading, *The Oregon Trail*.

"Isn't that book a little beyond your years?" he grumbled at his ten-year-old daughter.

"I find it fascinating," Ginny smiled. "All those courageous people who crossed a continent to start a new life, braving all sorts of dangers along the way."

"Her teachers say Ginny's reading is well advanced for her age," Claire added from her place on the sofa.

"It seems all Ginny reads about is pioneers and others who tramp about in the wilderness. She should be reading about ladies of society and her place in it."

Paul, who was also on the sofa reading a book, exchanged glances with Ginny and she replied, "Sometimes I think society is so boring."

"I think those people had a lot of courage," Paul added.

"I'm going to be a lady living in a big castle when I grow up," seven-year-old Victoria added as she ran up to Robert.

"I'm sure you will, little one, I'm sure you will," Robert said as he scooped his youngest daughter into his arms. "I expect your sister will be, also."

The maid informed them that dinner was served. At dinner Robert made an announcement. "We are all going to England at the end of March."

"To England," the others clamoured.

"What about the children and their schooling?" Claire worried.

"We'll only be gone a month. I am part of the team representing my company at a trade fair in London and besides, what better educational experience could the children have than a trip to London. The city is a virtual history book."

"Please, can we go?" Paul and Ginny both begged.

"Is England across the sea where the King lives?" Victoria chimed in.

"Yes, and I will show you his palace. There are Lords and Ladies everywhere." Robert smiled at his youngest daughter.

"I suppose in the light of things, the children can afford to miss school," Claire added. "All reports say they are doing well."

"I am arranging passage, second class on a liner leaving from Boston."

"Boston?" Claire asked.

"It is shorter by far than to go to Halifax and a better connection than Montreal. Besides, the children will get to see some of America along the way. It will take only about five days or so to reach Southampton and from there we'll take a train to London."

"Do you fancy being a lady in a big castle, Ginny?" Paul asked putting on a highbrow accent.

"I'd be charmed," Ginny added in a stiff tone of voice picking up a tea cup with her little finger properly curled. "Simply charmed."

Robert cleared his throat and replied, "Perhaps you will learn the value of your station and quit your foolish day-dreaming, Ginny."

Ginny's look grew serious and Paul remarked, "We were only kidding around, Father."

"You two are old enough to begin looking at life seriously. One day you'll be living in a mansion of your own."

"Really, Robert," Claire chided. "Let them be children for a while longer. They will decide their own course in life."

A rustling sound and the exclamation. "There's a damned rat!" issued from one of Paul's comrades, bringing him back to the present miserable conditions. Dale quicky produced a small hunting knife that he kept at his bunk and threw it at the vile creature. "Got him," he cried.

"You're getting pretty good at that," Curtis laughed as he saw the rat wiggling with the knife driven through its mid-section.

"I'm glad I brought my hunting knife with me overseas. It comes in handy." Then as he went over to the now dead rat, he picked it up by the knife skewer. "God. It's as big as a house cat."

"That's from all the carcasses it gets to feed on," Curtis remarked. "Get rid of it."

Dale tossed the rat out into the trench work with the comment, "Let its friends and relatives dispose of its body." Then he looked at Paul and said, "Do they have any rats in Toronto, Rich Kid?"

"Enough of this rich kid stuff already," Paul retorted. "You don't know what it is to be really rich. I remember the time when I was thirteen years old and we went to England with my father on business. We were invited to this Sir Wilfred Crawley's estate. An estate so vast and opulent that it made our Toronto home and our so-called social position seem insignificant. I mean this guy was real upper crust!" "Yeah, yeah," Dale replied.

"Tell us about it," Curtis interjected. "I always liked your rich kid stories."

"All right," Paul sighed..

Chapter Three

In the course of my father's duties over in London, he met and befriended a certain Sir Wilfred Crawley. I think he wanted to contract Father to handle some of his business affairs in Canada. Of course my father would never pass up an opportunity for a chance to earn more money, or especially to advance his social standing. In the course of events, Sir Wilfred invited our family to spend some time at his estate.

We arrived at Sir. Wilfred's Estate, via private railway coach, to the town of Avenbury, then via automobile to the actual estate. The automobile was a large expensive machine with polished brass trimmings, varnished wooden spoked wheels and leather seats. It was an open-air vehicle in which a glass partition separated the driver and lone occupant of the front seat from the passengers in the two facing back seats. We three Cunningham children were asked to take the rear-facing seat so the adults could have the forward-facing one. The countryside of west England is extremely beautiful.

"At least we can see where we've been," Paul said quietly to Ginny as they watched rolling countryside recede behind them.

"It's much like the countryside back home," Ginny smiled. They drove along a country lane shaded by an over-hang of spreading oak trees while weathered rail fences and hedges lined the sides of the road.

"I say Robert, do you have countryside like this over in Canada?" Sir Wilfred asked, overhearing Ginny's remark.

"Oh yes, in the part of Canada where we live, it is much like this," Robert replied.

"I always thought Canada a place of vast open plain and endless boreal forests," Wilfred replied.

"Much of it is," Robert chuckled, "but the civilized part

where we live in southern Ontario is hardwood forest.

"Indeed."

They turned into the estate proper between two stone gate posts, each of which held a large wrought-iron gate presently open. Ahead of them were vast manicured lawns abounding in carefully tended shrubbery, large bountiful flower gardens, and attendant tall beach and chestnut trees. The lawn on the right had a large gushing marble fountain in its midst and the one on the left had the hedge work arranged to create a large maze.

"Look at the maze," Ginny said. "I'll bet it would be fun to find one's way through that."

"Now Ginny," Claire said with a smile. "I'm sure Sir Wilfred doesn't want a bunch of children trampling all over his grounds.

"It's quite all right," Sir Wilfred chuckled. "The children will need their fresh air. My own children used to play about the grounds quite often. The labyrinth is a great attraction for all ages. If you're not tall enough to see over the hedge you can spend a lot of time working your way through it."

Then as they pulled up to a massive stone building that was three storeys high, this did not include the attic rooms beneath copper-sheeted roof. Wilfred said with a smile, "Welcome to my humble home."

As the others took in the scope of the building that dwarfed their ten-room house in Toronto to insignificance, Victoria said with wide eyes, "Do you live in a castle, Mr. Wilfred?"

"Hardly," Wilfred laughed. "You should see the estates of the real upper crust."

Presently, the front door opened and a tall thin man, who was impeccably dressed and whose wizened face seemed to be frozen in an expressionless mode, came to the car. Sir Wilfred stood up and addressed him.

"Charles, I should like to introduce our guests. Robert Cunningham, his charming wife, Claire, and their children, Paul, Virginia and Victoria. They are from Canada and I have invited them to stay over for a few days." Turning to Robert and Claire, he continued, "Charles is our butler and head of the household staff. He will attend to your every need."

"A pleasure to meet you and your family, sir," Charles said to Robert in his expressionless voice as he opened the automobile door. "I will strive to make your stay at Crawley Manner as comfortable and pleasurable as possible, sir and madam."

Sir Wilfred was first to step out of the car, followed by Robert. Charles assisted Claire and the girls out, while Paul climbed out on his own like the men. The driver removed the luggage from the rear of the automobile and set it by the front door, before taking his machine to the garage. Both Robert and the children instinctively moved to pick up their luggage, but Sir Wilfred interjected. "Charles and the upstairs maid will tend to your luggage. Come in, I am sure you are weary after the journey out here." Turning to Charles he said, "Since our guests are Canadians, perhaps they would like coffee instead of tea."

"Oh no," Robert's complexion turned ruddy as he replied, "Tea will be excellent, Canadians enjoy both beverages."

"As you wish, sir, both beverages will be served."

They were led into the immense main hall that was large enough to be a ballroom and no doubt used as such when the occasion demanded. The walls were adorned with exquisite oil paintings and tapestries, while fragile-looking sculptures adorned small delicately-constructed side tables along the walls. A broad flight of stairs led to the second storey that was bordered with a promenade that went completely around the main hall.

"It's, just like the ballroom in Cinderella," Victoria gasped, looking around the cavernous expanse with wide eyes.

"If the roof had turrets, it would be a real castle," Ginny added, also impressed with the enormous room.

As they were crossing the main hall a pleasant looking woman of middle age, dressed in a fine dress appeared. "My good wife, Lady Grace," Wilfred said.

Grace smiled and said in a welcome tone, "How do you do?"

"These are our guests of the Cunningham family from Canada that I wired you about," Wilfred said as he introduced them.

They exchanged greetings and Lady Grace said to Claire and the girls, with a concerned frown. "You must be exhausted after your journey. Do come into the parlour for refreshments."

Presently two maids appeared, dressed in their aprons and little round maid caps. Priscilla was introduced as the upstairs maid and would be responsible for their linen, laundry and preparing their baths. Daphne was introduced as the downstairs maid and would attend to their meals. Charles instructed Daphne to prepare refreshments for the guests.

As they headed for the parlour, Wilfred said to Robert, "I say, Robert, shall we step into the drawing-room for a smoke and a brandy? Your son may attend and I will get him one of the new carbonated beverages. What do they call them again?

"Soda pop," Paul replied.

The men went into the drawing-room, where Charles prepared brandy for the men and a soda pop for Paul. Robert was offered a Havana cigar while Wilfred loaded a large crooked pipe. Soon the room was full of the overpowering odour of tobacco smoke. As the men talked of politics, Paul noticed how Wilfred tended to refer to Canada as one of the colonies.

The women settled into the parlour to tea and crumpets. They were joined by Wilfred and Grace's daughter, Sarah Jane. Sarah had snobbish good looks and Ginny swore she kept her head tilted back at all times to assure that her nose was high in the air. She took a haughty condescending attitude to Ginny and Victoria, addressing them as if they were mere preschool children. When their home city of Toronto entered the conversation, she considered it to be a place of total insignificance. In her eyes, the only North American cities worthy of mention were Boston and New York, and *they* were compared unfavourably with London and Paris. As the conversation centred around fashion and topics of society, Ginny found it boring, and Sarah positively irritating. Sarah looked over Ginny's carefully picked attire as if she were wearing the clothes of a scullery maid. Though Ginny was only ten years old, she found the snobbish aloofness of Sarah unbearable. Thus, she excused herself at the earliest opportunity. Victoria stayed and eagerly absorbed as much of the society talk as her seven-year-old mind would allow. As she was younger she did not feel the condescending attitude the same way that Ginny did and if anything, viewed Sarah as a role model.

Meanwhile Wilfred's fifteen-year-old son, Jonathan, arrived home from his private boys school for the weekend. When he appeared at the drawing-room, Sir Wilfred introduced him to Paul. Then in suggesting that Jonathan entertain his Canadian guest, he said, "Perhaps you could take him riding."

Jonathan looked Paul over and finally said, "How are your equestrian skills?"

Paul looked at him curiously, then said, "Oh, you mean horseback riding."

"I suppose that is what you call it over there."

"I enjoy it very much. I've been to riding school."
Looking at Robert he continued, "May I go horseback riding,
Father?"

"Yes, you may," Robert said, "I presume Jonathan can
find a horse suitable for you."

"Yes, we have quite a selection in our stable," Wilfred
assured him. "Some of the people who come for the hunt can
barely get on a horse."

"Shall we go then," Jonathan said to Paul. Paul practi-
cally leapt to his feet with an opportunity to go riding and to
get out of the stuffy smoke-filled drawing-room.

"So, over there in Canada, I suppose you use the western
saddles?" Jonathan said as they walked across the grounds to
the stable.

"I've ridden with both," Paul replied. "I prefer the
western, but the academy taught us how to ride English."

"That's good, because I'm afraid there are no western
saddles in our tack room."

As they entered the large stable, the stableman was
there to meet them. "Are you going out riding, Master
Jonathan?"

"Yes, saddle up two horses. Pick one of the gentler
geldings for my guest." Then to Paul Jonathan said, "Come
to the tack room. Perhaps we can find some boots and attire
that will fit you."

So Paul got suited up in the proper attire of boots,
breaches and cap for English riding and was ready just as the
stableman brought out two horses. Jonathan was surprised
at how easily Paul mounted his horse and trotted toward the
gate. Soon they were racing across the vast estate grounds of
Sir Wilfred. At one point Jonathan spurred his horse to jump
over a hedge and to his surprise Paul followed suit.

"You ride quite well for a colonial, er should I say,

Canadian," Jonathan chucked as Paul drew up along side him after the jump.

"Canadian would be better," Paul replied. "We're quite proud of our nationhood."

"Yes. I understand that some of the more advanced colonies like Canada and Australia have become dominions now." Then in an abrupt change of topic Jonathan asked, "Have you ever been on a hunt?"

"Father plans to take me hunting with him next year."

"I mean a real hunt with horses and dogs. In pursuit of foxes and grouse."

"In Canada we usually hunt on foot and go away out into the forest for deer or moose."

"I say, you do things rather primitively over there, do you not?"

"I think it's more of a challenge than running some animal down with horses and dogs. Father says the real challenge is to stalk the animal and test one's skills as a hunter."

"I say, I shall have to come to Canada one day and try your way of hunting. Perhaps I can also learn to ride with a western saddle."

Paul smiled and they resumed their ride across the fields and woods of the estate.

When they returned and started for the house, Ginny came out to meet them. She wore an anxious look and asked her brother, "Paul, could you take me through the labyrinth?"

"Is this your little sister?" Jonathan asked.

"Yes, this is my sister, Ginny. I have an even smaller sister Vicky, somewhere in the house."

"Pleased to meet you," Jonathan smiled at Ginny in a condescending manner. "Ginny, did you say?"

"Yes, though everyone has been introducing me as

Virginia."

"That is the proper name, you know," Jonathan replied.

"Virginia is so formal," Ginny replied.

"Yes, of course, you Canadians are so earthy in your ways. Go ahead Paul, show her the labyrinth. I've got things to tend to. Perhaps tomorrow we can go to the shooting range."

"Sounds great, I've had shooting lessons also."

"I saw you out riding," Ginny said as they walked toward the labyrinth.

"Yes, it was nice of Jonathan to take me riding."

"You're lucky. I had to sit with the ladies and listen to boring conversations about fashions and society. They think Toronto is as far away as that place in Africa. . ."

"Timbuktu," Paul laughed.

"Yeah, Timbuktu, that's it. The only places in North America they've heard of are New York and Boston, and they don't *compare* to London."

"Of course not," Paul chuckled, as they reached the labyrinth. "We colonials are pretty crude."

"Jonathan says that too?" Ginny said.

"Oh yes, any place outside of England is one of the colonies to them, but I was getting him to say Canadian."

"You're lucky. At least he talks to you."

"Yes, but he still has the attitude that I am a mere child."

"Tell me about it," Ginny replied.

They came to a dead end within the maze and Paul stood on his tiptoes to see over it. "We need to go back to the last breach and turn left."

"I'm glad you can see over it. I'm lost."

"So what about Vicky?" Paul continued. "She's not bored."

"She's lapping it up. She wants to be a lady of society

when she grows up, and Sarah Jane has taken her under wing."

"And you don't?" Paul laughed.

"It seems so stuffy, and Sarah Jane looks right through me as if I were one of the maids," Ginny replied. "I think all those pioneers who ran away from society that I read about, had a more interesting life."

"A lot harder one too, I would imagine" Paul added. They were now deep within the labyrinth.

"I suppose," Ginny sighed. "Do you know where we are going?"

Again Paul stood on his tiptoes. "We're almost out."

A few moments later they emerged from the other end of the labyrinth.

"That was easy," Ginny replied. "Just like everything else in our world."

"Oh Ginny, for a ten-year-old, you seem so knowing for your years."

"Not as wise as you though," Ginny added, smiling at her brother.

"Oh, dear sister," Paul said as he put an arm around Ginny and squeezed her for a moment. "We are two of a kind."

Ginny smiled up at her brother.

If Paul was able to find an outlet to pass his time at Sir Wilfred's estate by riding and shooting, and Victoria was able to attach herself as a young protege of Sarah Jane, Ginny was bored to tears. She tried to spend time in Sir Wilfred's huge library, but found most of the great selection of leather-bound books unappealing and so delicate that she was reminded to handle them with great care. Often she looked longingly out the window at Paul and Jonathan riding across the fields on horseback wishing she could be with them. Ginny then moved to exploring the vast grounds. Sometimes she sat dreamily by the fountain or tried her hand at going through the labyrinth on her own. All too soon though, she figured out how easy it was to find her own way through the maze.

On her third afternoon there, Ginny found her way to a cluster of cottages near the stables. These were the homes of the outside staff that maintained the estate beyond the walls of the great house. Ginny strolled down the road that ran through the midst of the cottage cluster and the pleasant smell of wood smoke was in the air. Women folk and their children could be seen busily doing laundry or tending their small garden plots. A girl about Ginny's age with long brown hair and dressed in a simple pinafore came down the road from the opposite direction.

"Hello," Ginny smiled.

"Hello madam," the girl replied as they stopped in the middle of the road.

"There is no need to call me madam. I am probably no older than you," Ginny laughed.

"We are told that we must address all people from the big house in a proper manner."

"I am only a guest. I am from Canada."

"From Canada?" the girl was wide-eyed at having met a real Canadian.

"From Toronto. What is your name?"

"Molly. My real name is Margaret, but they call me Molly," the girl replied.

Ginny laughed and replied, "My real name is Virginia, but they call me Ginny, though the people of the house insist on calling me Virginia."

"Ginny is a nice name."

"Come along now, Molly," said a terse female voice. They turned and a stout middle-aged woman, presumably Molly's mother, emerged from one of the cottages. Speaking with an Irish lilt she said, "We have plenty of work to be doin', there's no time for dawdlin'" Then turning to Ginny, the woman said, "Is there anything we can help you with ma'am?"

"No, I just went for a walk to see what was down here," Ginny replied pleasantly.

"We are the folk that look after the estate," the woman replied. "No one from the house comes here unless it is to give orders." Then to Molly she added, "Go on in, child, and start scrubbin' the floor."

"Goodbye," Molly said in a doleful tone as she turned to go into a nearby cottage.

"Goodbye Molly," Ginny replied. "I'll see you again."

"I'm sorry ma'am, if me daughter was botherin' you, but ye shouldn't be down here."

"I want to be her friend," Ginny said. "She is a lot friendlier than Lady Sarah."

The woman gave a fleeting smile then quickly replied, "Run along now, away back up to the big house, to yer own kind." The woman turned and followed Molly into the house.

Ginny slowly walked back to the grounds of the big house to the bench beside the fountain. Then she sat to contemplate, *'What did they mean, her own kind? Was it so wrong to want to be friendly with someone of a lower station?'*

Nonetheless, the following day, Ginny went back down to the cottages to seek out Molly.

She found Molly in a small vegetable garden beside the cottage, weeding the potato crop.

"Hi Molly," Ginny called from over the wicker fence.

Molly looked up with a smile and replied, "Hello, Ginny."

"You still have work to do?"

"I always have work to do. It is the lot of us poor folk to work."

"May I come in and join you?" Ginny asked.

Molly straightened up and looked at her. "You're a lady. You enjoy the work that others do." Then with a wry look she added, "You might get yer dress dirty."

"I have plenty of others." Ginny found the gate and let herself into the small cottage plot.

Molly looked fearfully around and said in a low voice, "Don't let anyone from the big house see you here, or the lot of us will be in trouble."

Molly dropped to her knees and resumed weeding. Ginny also knelt down and for the first time learned to tell the difference between vegetables and weeds as she helped pluck the latter out. Somehow the feel of the warm earth in her hands seemed invigorating. Soon the two girls were laughing as they chattered and plucked weeds. Social barriers began to dissolve as they became merely two preteen age girls developing a sense of friendship. At one point Molly's mother came to the doorway. She was about to intervene on behalf of this for-bidden social mixing, but resigned with a great sigh and a hand on her hip as she watched the two girls having an enjoyable time together.

When the weeding was done, Molly invited Ginny to come in for a cup of tea. It was a small neatly-kept cottage with stone walls and a slate tiled roof. The main room had a hearth on one side and two lead-off bedrooms from the other. A simple ladder led to a loft above. A small fire was crackling in the hearth with a black kettle hanging above the flame. Ginny looked around the room with its simple wooden furniture and a spinning wheel in one corner. It seemed so rustic and homey compared to the vast sterile rooms of the main house.

"Welcome to our simple home, Miss," her mother smiled. "It is a far cry from the big house, but it is all we got."

"Your house is nice, Ma'am," Ginny replied. "The big house is so big, I get lost most of the time."

"Do ye drink tea, Madam?" Molly's mother asked.

"You may call me Ginny," Ginny replied. "Everyone in the house either calls me Madam or Virginia. Yes, I am allowed a cup of tea."

"Ginny is a common name for someone of upper class, is it not?" Molly's mother replied.

"I've always been called Ginny. My father is only a lawyer from Canada, we are guests of a Lord."

"Indeed you are. Canada did you say? That's away across the sea."

Presently a middle-aged man came into the house as Molly's mother set out the teacups and a platter of biscuits. He looked curiously at the well-dressed Ginny, and Molly explained. "This is my friend, Ginny, from Canada. Ginny, this is my Da'."

"From Canada, ye say? Are ye per chance a guest at the big house?"

"Yes," Ginny said in a low voice.

"What are ye doin' a way down here?"

"I was bored so I came down here and made friends with Molly."

"And what does the Master or your father say about that?"

"They don't know."

He looked at his wife for an explanation.

"Young Ginny met Molly on the road beside the cottage yesterday. I tried to tell her she should be goin', but she wants to be friends with our Molly. This mornin' I found the pair of them in the garden pullin' weeds. "

"It's a friendship best kept secret," he said with a wink. "If the Master finds out yer down here havin' tea wit' the likes of us, we'll all be in trouble. I'll escort ye back after the tea."

After the midday tea, Ginny reluctantly said farewell

to Molly as her father walked her back to the grounds. Ginny chatted amicably with him as he explained his job as the gardener who planted and maintained the labyrinth.

They were nearly at the door when Robert and Sir Wilfred appeared.

"The lass found her way down to the cottages, sir" he said meekly. "So I escorted her back."

"Thank you, Timothy. You may carry on with your duties," Sir Wilfred said without expression.

After Timothy had walked away, Robert turned to Ginny. "What were you doing down there among the cottages?"

"I was bored and went for a walk," Ginny replied mildly.

"You were seen down there both yesterday and today," he continued, ever sternly.

"I have a new friend down there. Her name is Molly."

"You can't have friends down there," Robert admonished. "You are not to associate with those people."

"Why Father?" Ginny was in tears.

"They are of a much lower station than us, mere hired help for the estate. You should be like your sister and spend your time with Sarah Jane and learn the social graces of a lady."

'On how to be a snob,' Ginny thought. "It is so boring at the house," Ginny protested.

"Now go on in the house. I don't want to see you go off the front grounds again."

Ginny went into the house and straight to her bed for a good long cry. She felt that she had found a good friend in Molly, but some unfathomable social barrier had been thrust in her way.

The Cunningham family left the following morning to return to Canada. As they were about to go out the front gate, Ginny saw Molly gathering the trimmings as her father was busy clipping the hedges. As their eyes met Ginny waved frantically in spite of her scowling father. Molly waved briefly then turned away. Ginny sank back down in her seat heavily. Molly knew her place in the social order; Ginny did not understand why there needed to be social barriers.

*   *   *

The call came for lights out in five minutes. All the squad members scrambled to get ready for bed and Paul put his letters in his kit bag and his food items in a metal container. As he lay in his bunk listening to the dull explosions of the cannons exchanging fire, Paul again thought back. How indeed, had he ended up in the middle of this insanity and carnage?

Chapter Four

Paul recalled those heady days of June 1914. The newspapers were plastered with headlines about the Archduke of Austria-Hungary and his wife being assassinated by a Serbian terrorist. This was followed by a flurry of diplomatic scurrying and sabre-rattling by major European powers.

"Do you think there will be a war, Father?" Paul asked one night at dinner as the situation in Europe continued to deteriorate.

"I suppose if those nations on the continent don't come to their senses soon, some kind of a war will occur with Germany right in the middle of it."

"I was reading in the papers," Paul continued, "that, if Austria attacks Serbia, Russia will attack Austria, if Russia attacks Austria, Germany will attack Russia, and if Germany attacks Russia, France will attack Germany."

"Just like a row of dominoes," Ginny added.

"Yeah," Robert sighed.

"Will Canada get involved?" Claire worried.

"If Britain gets involved Canada will be involved."

"Aren't we an independent country?" Ginny asked.

Paul snorted and replied, "We are allowed to run our own business internally, but our foreign affairs are still run by the British."[1]

"So if England declares war, Canada will automatically be involved then?" Claire asked.

"Yes my dear."

"Who cares about some war," eleven-year-old Victoria complained. "When are we going to our summer cottage?"

---

[1] Even though Canada considers that its nationhood began with Confederation in 1867, Canada did not become a truly independent nation until the Statute of Westminister in 1932.

"We will be going for a full month starting on the first of July," Robert smiled.

"We'll celebrate Dominion Day at the cabin then," Claire said.

"Yes, my dear. We'll be far away from all this talk of war and such."

"I can't get far enough away," Claire added.

Even in their retreat at the northern end of the Niagara peninsula near the Canadian Shield, the newspapers found their way to the Cunningham family. One day in early August near the end of their vacation, Paul came running breathlessly into the cabin with the newspaper that Robert had sent him to fetch.

"It's war, Father, it's war!" he cried breathlessly.

Robert picked up the paper and across the front page in huge letters was the word WAR.

Full-scale war had erupted in Europe. The paper went on to explain that as the German armies swept through Belgium on their way to attack France, the British entered the fray on the pretext that Germany had violated Belgian neutrality. In Ottawa, Prime Minister Borden reiterated Canada's commitment to the British Empire and the call went out for volunteers to join the Army to stop the Hun, as the Germans were now called, from overrunning France. Robert read each word seriously, Paul felt a certain elation, and Claire was horrified.

"If this war is still on when I'm old enough, I'm joining up," Paul declared that night as they ate supper at the cabin.

"Oh, heaven forbid," Claire said, her eyes rolling upward.

"I think the war will be over by then," Robert said to Claire. "Paul is only seventeen." And to Paul he said, "I think your college education is more important. The Prime Minister is only asking for volunteers and there are plenty of others from lower stations to fill the ranks."

"Are we too good to fight for our country?" Paul said with his voice rising.

"There are lots of way to help our country with the war besides marching into battle and getting yourself killed," Robert insisted.

"What if I want to go into battle?" Paul shouted.

"Why would anyone want go to war and get killed?" Victoria wondered.

"Exactly," Robert declared. "I don't want to hear any more about you wanting to join the Army. It is upsetting your mother. You will go on to university like we planned."

"Like you planned," Paul said with an agitated voice. "It is always what you planned."

Paul got up and abruptly left the table despite Robert's demands that he stay.

"No son of mine is going to be crawling around in the mud with the sons of farmers and immigrants."

"Oh Robert," Claire said. "Paul is young. Unfortunately, there seems to be a certain male excitement about the war."

"I suppose," Robert sighed heavily.

"I'll go and talk to him," Ginny offered.

"You do that, dear," Claire smiled. "You two seem to have a good rapport.

Ginny found Paul sitting at a bench down by the lake, still fuming. She sat down quietly beside him and smiled when he looked at her.

"Father is so demanding," Paul grumbled. "Everything has to be his way. Doesn't he know that I have a mind of my own?"

"I know," Ginny smiled. "I heard him talking to Mother last night and he was stressing how I should soon be introduced as a proper lady of society. So I can be so *charming*," Ginny added with a put-on tone of voice.

Paul laughed. "So what do you think about the idea of

me joining up when I'm old enough?"

"Well, dear brother," Ginny said. "I'd be worried sick the whole time you were over there."

"I'll come back. I said I'd always be here for you."

"Yes, you did. I just hope the war is over before you are old enough."

"You too, eh," Paul said becoming serious and looking away from his sister. "Just like the others."

"I'll support whatever you decide, Paul," Ginny said, grasping his arm. "Just as I trust you'll support me."

"Support you?"

"I have no intention of becoming a debutant," Ginny said. "Living in a mansion, having tea parties with nothing to talk about but my clothing, vacation plans and idle gossip. Remember that time when we were in England and I was forbidden to be friends with Molly, the gardener's daughter?"

"Yes."

Well, I resolved from that day forward that I want to live in a world where I can be friends with whomever I so choose, be they rich or poor."

"What are you planning to do then? Live on a homestead?"

"That is entirely possible," Ginny laughed. "I've been thinking about a career as a school teacher or nurse. Once I have been properly trained, I'll go out west."

"Father would be positively furious," Paul laughed. "I plan to get as far away from Toronto as possible also. I kind of thought of going to Vancouver."

"I suppose we shouldn't be too hard on Father, he does love us and thinks he has our best interests at heart," Ginny replied as her reflection of her father mellowed.

"Yes, I suppose he does," Paul sighed heavily. "If he'd just let us have some input into what our best interests are."

"Come let's go back to the house," Ginny smiled, rising and tugging at Paul. "Try to avoid mentioning joining the Army at least until you are old enough."

"You are beautiful, dear sister," Paul smiled, as he got up. "I am so fortunate to have a sister like you. I support you Ginny, wherever you go or whatever you do in life I will be there with you in spirit if not in body."

Ginny smiled radiantly at her brother and hugged him with one arm.

Paul graduated from secondary school the following year and the war was still on and locked in bloody stalemate. The war was slowly expanding with Italy joining the allies and the empire of the Ottoman Turks throwing in their lot with Germany and Austria, bringing the war to the Mediterranean and the Middle East. British Empire forces, composed mainly of Australians, had taken a severe mauling in a failed assault against the Turks at Gallipoli. The newspapers, while downplaying the Gallipoli disaster, boasted of the Canadian Army holding the line at Ypres as the Germans introduced deadly chlorine gas as a weapon of war. The lethal gas had caused other soldiers to flee in its path, and by staying put on the high ground the Canadians had prevented a German breakthrough.

Once again Paul was hit with a patriotic urge to join up and once again he brought it up at supper. "Now that I am graduated from high school, and am eighteen years old. I think it is time I joined up to serve our country."

"What!" Robert exclaimed. Ginny's mouth dropped and Claire let out an almost inaudible cry."

"I want to serve our country. I feel great pride in the Canadian Army after Ypres."

"You know how I feel about that," Robert said sharply. "I have already arranged for you to attend university."

"What about me and what I want to do?"

"You will get a degree first. Maybe by that time the war will be over."

"Do I at least get to choose what I want to study, or did you arrange that too?" Paul sneered at his father.

"I take exception to your tone of voice," Robert said sharply.

"I take exception to you dictating every step of my life," Paul argued.

"Now Paul," Claire interjected. "It is your father you are talking to and he has your best interests at heart."

"How does he know my best interests? He has never asked me what my interests are. He has always told me."

"You know, my company and several others are involved in the war effort," Robert said in a softer tone. "You could get a war-related job here and still be serving your country."

"And be thought a coward for staying home," Paul added.

"Well, if you must go to the army, get a non-combatant job in ordinance or something. And above all, take officer's training."

"There you go again," Paul said, his voice rising.

"I think you should go to college first," Claire added quietly. "At least for next year."

"I'll think about it," Paul said, excusing himself from the table.

"You don't suppose he's foolish enough to join the army do you?" Claire wondered.

"Ah, this damned war has everyone fired up. The longer it goes on, the more tempting it is for him to want to join," Robert replied. "If he does try to join, I'll try to get him shunted off to a non-combatant role and with any luck at all he won't even have to leave Canada."

"Do you really think you can pull the right strings?"

"I will look seriously into it because I fear we can't hold him off forever."

"Do what you can dear. I don't want our son going over there to die on some battlefield."

"Neither do I, dear, neither do I."

"Why would Paul want to go to war?" Victoria wondered.

"Who knows?" Robert replied with a shrug.

Ginny quietly excused herself from the table to seek out her brother. She found him in the front parlour staring out the window at the park across the street. As if sensing her approach Paul turned to face Ginny and said abruptly. "I suppose you're going to plea for me to stay home also."

"What you decide to do with your life, Paul, is your affair," Ginny replied. "Come, let's go for a walk in the park. It is a beautiful evening."

"Yes, it is a little stuffy in here," Paul grinned crookedly. Ginny smiled back as they moved toward the door.

"What should I do, Ginny?," Paul asked as they walked along through the park. "Stay home like a coward and hide behind Father?"

"There are plenty of well-to-do young men who would," Ginny replied.

"I'm not well-to-do," Paul said in a sharp tone. "Father is well-to-do, or so he thinks. If I ever become well-to-do it will be by my own hand, not with his money."

"I know the feeling," Ginny smiled, and then putting on a phoney air she continued. "If I am to become a debutant, it will be because I want to, not because Father or Mother wish it."

"Oh, Ginny, we are so like-minded," Paul laughed. "We should have been twins." Then in a sober tone he added, "Then you won't mind if I run away and join the army?"

"Of course I mind," Ginny said. "I would probably not sleep at night worrying about you on some battlefield with the whole German Army shooting at you. But then again, you must follow your destiny and if that destiny takes you to the front, then so be it."

"Oh, Ginny, you are beautiful, and so sensible for someone who is only fifteen."

"I was born on the first day of the century and because of that, Father says I have a special destiny."

"I'm sure you have dear sister. I'm sure you have."

"One thing more, Paul, while I'll not try to talk you out of joining up, wait a few months."

"Why? I am eighteen so I can join if I wish."

"If you join now, Father told Mother that he will use his influence to get you a safe army job."

"He did, did he," Paul said angrily. "He won't even let me join the army on my own terms."

"That's why you should wait and go through the ruse of going to college," Ginny said. "Join later when his guard is down."

"You really don't want me to go, do you?" Paul grinned.

"Of course not. I want you to be around for a while yet."

"I'll be back," Paul assured her. "I said I'd always be here for you and I always will."

Ginny smiled.

"For your sake and your sake alone, I will stay and enroll in college at least for this semester. After that I will make no promises."

"After that I will not try to talk you into staying," Ginny replied with misty eyes. "I will just pray for your return."

"God bless you, Ginny," Paul choked as he squeezed her with one arm.

Paul enrolled in university that following autumn, a move that pleased his parents very much. Robert was disappointed, however, that Paul enrolled in general courses rather than plunging straight into law or commerce. The War continued onward and while the casualty lists grew, everyone still talked of the glory of it all. Paul saw classmates drift away one by one although many from the richer families either went in for officers or non-combatant roles. The pull to join up was becoming irresistible.

Instead of returning to class for the new semester at the beginning of 1916, Paul found his way to a recruiting office. It was the fifth of January and Paul had turned nineteen the previous day. He signed the papers then took his oath to serve God, His Majesty King George V of the British Empire, and the Dominion of Canada. Paul did not go home that night, but stayed in a hotel and sent a note saying he was staying over with a friend. In his hotel room he composed letters both to his parents and Ginny that he planned to mail once he was at training camp.

To his parents, Paul wrote:

Dear Mom and Dad.

I have gone against your wishes and joined the army as I could no longer resist the patriotic call to duty. Although I know that you will be angry, Father, I must do this on my own terms and I forbid you to intervene. If I should suddenly find myself pulled out of the army, or shunted off to a non-combatant role, I will assume that you are still trying to dictate my life and act accordingly. By that, I mean I will move far away from Toronto and go down to one of the lower stations that you despise, by living out my life as a farmer, lumberjack or a miner. So please let me do what my destiny is calling me to do.

Mother, I know you will be worried sick about my going overseas, but fear not, I fully intend to survive this war as I made a promise to Ginny. When it is over I will come home and maybe even be ready for a respectable career that will be acceptable to Father. So farewell for now and God bless.

Love From Your Son
Paul

"The boy is insane," Robert ranted, upon reading the letter. "He has gone off to join the army. I must try to put a stop to this."

"May I see the letter?" Claire asked calmly, although her heart was pounding with the sheer terror of her son going off to war.

As Claire read, Robert paced and fumed about what steps he must take to get Paul out of the army or moved to a desk job

Finally Claire put down the letter and said, "Did you really read this letter?"

Robert glanced sharply at her.

"It says that if he finds that his proposed army career is interfered with, he will run away and live out his life in the working class."

"Ha!" Robert snorted. "If he tries his hand at that, he'll soon find their way of life too hard and miserable."

"But he may disassociate himself from us, whatever he does."

"I would take what Paul says very seriously," Ginny said gravely. She was also holding a letter from Paul. "Read what Paul wrote to me."

Dear Ginny,

Depending on whose letter was opened first you will learn that I have enlisted in the army. Mother and probably you will be horrified and Father will be furious. Father will probably fume and rant and threaten to interfere with my decision in some way, but he would be wise to contain his disappointment and consider all that has been said and done. I have made this momentous decision for two very important reasons.

One. Our country and the British Empire are at war

and as a true patriot I can no longer resist the call. I felt proud today as I stood and swore my service to His Majesty King George V and the Dominion of Canada, and I will allow nothing to reverse that oath.

Two. I must do this to prove my worth as a man, a man who has the right to make his own decisions. While I know my father loves me very much and believes he has my best interests at heart, he needs also to realize that I am of age and must seek my own destiny. If that destiny means that I ultimately seek a lifestyle and profession that meets with Father's approval, so be it. If it means that I go down to the lower stations that he so despises, then he must respect that decision also. For now though, duty is calling and if I sense that my decision is being tampered with, I will make good the warning I gave to him.

As for you dear sister, I believe you understand my decision and will stand by me. I know that you will be worried sick, but remember my promise that I will always be here for you.
Your Beloved Brother
Paul

Robert took the letter from Ginny and read. As he read, he slowly sank into a nearby chair.

"Are you going to do something to stop our son from going away to war?" Claire asked anxiously.

"No," Robert replied in a small voice as he handed her the letter.

"Oh my God, Robert," she finally said as she read the letter and handed it back to Ginny. "Perhaps you should have given him more leeway instead of dictating his life. Then perhaps he would not have made this awful decision so suddenly."

"Perhaps," Robert sighed. "This confounded war is

slowly sucking us all in like a whirlpool. They said it would be over in six months and that was two years ago."

"What are we going to do?" was Claire's anxious reply.

"Wish him well and hope he survives," Robert said. "What else can we do?"

Claire looked at Ginny for support and she replied, "I'm worried too, but Father is right. Paul must find his destiny."

Chapter Five

Paul was taken to training camp somewhere in the Canadian Shield of northern Ontario. There he was issued two uniforms, a rifle, and attendant combat gear. Then he was sent to bunk with the squad of trainees in a large tent that never seemed to warm enough in the cold wintery weather. He was thrown in with a squad of recruits picked from other areas primarily the Lakehead and Manitoba. Most of the others of his squad regarded him cooly in spite of efforts to be friendly. Their rough manner with slang and profanity-filled accents suggested they were from those lower stations with which his father was so obsessed. They in turn, recognized his polished manner of speaking that suggested he had been taught in private schools. Naive in many ways of the world beyond his cloistered circle, Paul was soon tricked into revealing what they had suspected of his background and thereafter he was taunted as Rich Kid. Paul would try to explain that his father was rich, not he, and this aggravated the situation.

"If I wanted to behave like a rich kid, I would have become an officer. Or perhaps stayed out of the army altogether like many of my peers."

"Perhaps I'd be an officer or a coward." one of his tormentor's named Curtis Smith said, mimicking Paul's speech inflection. Curtis was a tall, rugged-looking man in his mid-twenties and, as one with a natural gift as a leader, was Paul's chief tormenter. Bob White was a wanly handsome man and natural follower from Sudbury Ontario as was his close friend, Jim Jones. While most of the squad members were just plain indifferent, Bob White, Jim Jones and ring leader Curtis Smith were merciless. Paul was taunted and teased. His gear and bed were often tampered with, or he might just be tripped and sent sprawling.

Often joining this trio was a fourth recruit, Dale Chalmers. Dale Chalmers was one of those short guys with curly hair and a perpetual impish grin who was forever speaking out of turn. Never the instigator but always the contributor, Dale often chimed in with his own barbs when opportunity provided. Unlike Paul who only wished that Curtis and his friends would leave him alone, Dale sought mightily to be part of their group. Dale was short-statured, the shortest man in their squad, and they often taunted him calling him Shorty or Runt, and would push him out of the way, but Dale was irrepressible.

Even the sergeant who was impartial when he barked his orders on the parade square, called Paul, Rich Kid. When the squad was lined up for inspection with the sharp-eyed sergeant looking for a point of contention, it was always Paul's puttees.

"Cunningham, your puttees are on crooked!" he would yell. "Straighten them on the double."

Humiliated, Paul would quickly kneel down, unwind the strips of cloth from around the calves of his legs that made up his puttees, then rewind them again. Sometimes his tormentors would snicker and if the sharp eye of the sergeant spotted that person, usually Dale or Jim, they might be ordered to do push-ups or sent to jog around the parade square.

One night his tormentors tried a new tack. They feigned friendship and invited him over to their corner of the barracks.

"Say, Rich Kid," Curtis swaggered. "It's time to become one of the boys." He slapped Paul on the back so hard that Paul winced.

Bob White said, "It's time you had a smoke with the boys." He offered one of the cheap cigars of the type he liked to smoke while relaxing.

"I don't smoke," Paul replied.

"Come on, you gotta try," Bob continued as he waved the

cigar in Paul's face. "All soldiers smoke sooner or later."

"Yeah, there are three things soldiers do besides fight the enemy," Jim added with a laugh. "Do you know what they are?"

"No," Paul said in a low voice.

"They smoke, they drink, and they chase loose women."

The others all guffawed.

"Ain't you ever heard that a whore is a soldier's best friend," Curtis added while the others laughed uproariously.

"You sure are naive for a rich boy. Have this cigar, if you're gonna be one of the boys, yuh gotta act like one of 'em. Here take it."

Paul reluctantly took the cigar in his mouth and Bob lit it. He felt that if he was to ever make peace with his tormentors, he would have to go along with them. After a few puffs he coughed and sputtered to the amusement of the others.

"Maybe I should start with cigarettes," he choked as he handed the cigar back.

"Now for the second thing," Curtis said as he produced a flask of whiskey from his footlocker.

"You brought booze in here?" Paul said incredulously.

"Yeah, so what?" Curtis replied with a growl. "Are you gonna squeal on me?"

"Rich kids don't squeal," Paul added quickly.

"That's good, so prove it by taking the first drink," Curtis said as he uncorked the bottle.

Paul reluctantly took a drink and Curtis cast a menacing look around to the others in the squad tent not involved. They all turned away, suggesting that they would feign ignorance if ever questioned about liquor in the barracks.

Dale chimed in, "What about me? I'll take a swallow of your booze." He rose from his bunk and came over to them.

"Oh, go sit down," Bob said pushing him hard enough to cause Dale to fall back on his own bunk. "There isn't enough whiskey for a runt to have any."

Nonetheless, Dale sat on the edge of his bunk watching the activity, acting as if he were fully involved. Instead of feeling empathy for Paul, who was being set up, he viewed the taunting of Paul as taking their attentions away from deriding him.

Paul choked down a swallow of strong whiskey. The flask was passed around with each taking a small drink before it was passed back to Paul whereupon he was induced to take another large drink. By the time the contents of the flask were consumed, Paul was quite drunk and reduced to babbling and giggling about who Curtis said was a soldier's best friend.

"Hey Rich Kid," Curtis laughed with an arm around Paul's shoulder.

"Paul, the name's Paul," Paul slurred.

"Hey Paulsy walsy," he continued. "There's one more thing to do before you pass initiation."

"Wha-s that?" Paul slurred.

"Yuh gotta sneak over to the mess kitchen and steal us a pan of white buns. The officers always get white buns with their supper, but us grunts never get any. I know the cook made some today."

"The mess," Paul slurred. "It's a real mess." He trailed off into a giggle.

Curtis laughed. "Just go do it," he urged, "and hide the bottle in a garbage bin along the way."

"To the mess," Paul slurred as he staggered out the door with the bottle in hand. Outside the mess, he found a large waste bin and there, with much effort, he stuffed the bottle deep down in the garbage. He stumbled his way through the mess, giggling as he crashed into a number of things and upset a stack of dishes, causing a loud clatter of smashing earthenware. He was still crashing around in the kitchen trying to find where the bread was kept when the cook appeared with a lantern and two military police.

"What the hell is going on in my kitchen?" he demanded.

"The boys want a snack," Paul giggled.

"He's drunk out of his mind," the cook said to the MP. "Take him away."

"Okay, what the hell happened last night?" the sergeant demanded as he interrogated Paul the following morning.

"I was drunk, sir," Paul admitted since denial would be futile.

"That's obvious. Where did you get the booze?"

"I found it, sir."

"Found it, indeed. You know that no liquor is allowed in the barracks."

"Yes sir."

"Was anyone else involved."

Paul was silent.

"They said when they found you that you were getting a snack for the boys. Was Curtis Smith or Bob White involved?"

Paul remained silent.

"I know they torment you, so why cover for them?"

"I'm not covering, sir."

"Well, I don't know what else you'd call it. You know it would go easier for you if you told me where you really got the stuff."

"I told you I found it, sir."

"Where did you put the bottle?"

"I don't remember."

"Well, seeing you can't remember and seem to like being in the kitchen, I am sending you to kitchen duty for an undetermined length of time, beginning immediately. Dismissed."

So Paul was sent to the kitchen where he spent his time washing dishes and peeling potatoes. The cook was very demanding about having his cookware spotlessly clean. The rest of the squad was lectured in a lineup by the sergeant. He made no secret of his suspicion about the involvement of Paul's tormentors. The squad was sent to root through all the garbage containers on the base until the offending bottle was found, then they were interrogated again, and finally sent on a grueling hike.

When Paul returned to his bunk from kitchen duty that night, Curtis, Bob and Jim were waiting for him. They accused him of being a squealer and began shoving him around menacingly. When Paul tried to defend himself he was punched in the face. As Paul stepped backwards, Dale tripped him. What's the matter, Rich Kid, can't you even stand up?" he leered. He then looked for approval from Curtis for his action, but the others all ignored him.

The uproar in the barracks soon brought the sergeant just as Paul was stumbling back to his bunk with a bruised and bleeding mouth.

The squad was called to attention and as the sergeant eyed them all over, he stopped at Paul.

"Cunningham, what happened to your face?"

"I stumbled coming through the door, sir" Paul answered directly.

"Some stumble," he said sharply. "I want you all to settle down and not another peep out of you. As far as I'm concerned, it's lights out for the night."

There were groans from some who hoped to read for another half-hour until the usual time for lights out. When the sergeant left, Curtis said to Paul, "I'm glad for your sake, Rich Boy, that you didn't squeal."

Paul made no comment.

The following morning at reveille, Paul's injuries had expanded to a black eye and swollen lip. The sergeant called him out to come to his office when the others were dismissed.

"You didn't get a black eye and fat lip falling through the doorway, did you?"

"No sir, I mean, I don't know, sir."

"Suppose I offered to transfer you to another outfit in exchange for information on both who gave you the black eye and who got you drunk that night. Bullying is not tolerated any more than drinking in the barracks or fighting with each other."

"I don't want a transfer sir. I'd be running away from my problems."

"I see. How much tormenting are you prepared to put up with?"

"If I am to be any good at fighting the Hun, sir, I must learn to deal with my comrades here, sir."

"I see. However, since you won't cooperate, I have no choice but to keep you on kitchen duty for the foreseeable future, as well as spending time on the parade square. Is that clear?"

"Yes, sir."

"Dismissed."

When the squad minus Paul was lined up for morning inspection, the sergeant lectured them again.

"You may think it is funny to torture a man because he appears different. You may envy him because he came from a well-to-do family, but you forget that he volunteered to be a soldier like you. He could have taken the easy route and stayed out of the army, or got a desk job, but he chose to fight for his country. He could even still put in to be an officer, then come back to haunt you. You know, I offered to transfer him to a different outfit in exchange for information on the beating and the booze. He refused and said he would have to solve his own problems if he was ever to be a good enough soldier to fight the Hun. Right now, I would much rather be in the trenches with him than any one of you. Don't you think, Smith!" he shouted in Curtis's face.

"Yes, sir," Curtis replied in a small voice.

"You wouldn't know anything about how he got a black eye, would you?" the sergeant continued mercilessly.

"No, sir."

"Funny, he said the same thing when I asked him."

"What about the bottle in the barracks, Mr. White?" he shouted at Bob White.

"I don't know, sir."

"Funny how an empty whiskey bottle appears in the garbage, a soldier is found drunk one night and beaten the next, and nobody knows anything." Then continuing as he paced in front of his squad that was standing at rigid attention. "If we are to beat the Hun we must pull together and not worry about being rich or poor. We are all Canadians, so we must act like Canadians. To get you to appreciate the value of teamwork we are going on a twenty-mile hike with full gear." The sergeant turned on his heel and cried, "Fall out."

Curtis was first to break. He had felt guilty about striking Paul after getting him into trouble with the liquor. As they were about to march he turned suddenly to the sergeant and said, "Permission to help Private Cunningham with his kitchen duties, *sir*."

The sergeant cried halt and then spoke to Curtis with a wry grin. "Is that a confession, soldier?"

"Perhaps Private Cunningham is not all to blame, sir."

"Permission granted. You will serve the same length of kitchen duty as Cunningham."

"Yes, sir," Curtis smiled. He stepped out of rank to deposit his gear to join Paul at kitchen duty.

"Stay put," the sergeant said.

"I would like to help too, sir," Bob White suddenly said.

"And me too," Jimmy Jones added.

Dale's face quavered for a moment but he remained silent. He felt, though he was an accessory, he was not an instigator

"By God, we'll make soldiers out of you guys yet," the Sergeant grinned. "However, there is no room left in the kitchen, so you two will be on latrine duty."

"Yes, sir," they said in unison.

"We will all do that hike first though,"

"Yes, sir," they replied in unison again.

Paul was busy scrubbing out the large pot used for soup at the noonday meal when he was surprised to hear Curtis reporting for kitchen duty. The cook gruffly acknowledged, then sent him to help Paul with the scrubbing of the large enamel pots with dire warnings not to drop any and chip the enamel.

"What are you doing here?" Paul asked without expression.

"I thought you needed a hand," Curtis replied nonchalantly.

"I'm doing rather well on my own," Paul continued coldly.

Curtis rolled up his sleeves and reached into the hot water for a pot to scrub. They scrubbed in silence for a few moments, then Paul finally said, "So what did you do to end up washing dishes with the rich kid?"

Curtis cleared his throat and replied, "I had a bad attack of conscience after the sergeant got through with us this morning."

Paul smiled crookedly and asked, "What about Bob and Jim?"

"They're on latrine duty," Curtis laughed.

"Indeed. They had an attack of conscience also?"

"And Dale."

"The runt," Curtis snorted. "He was too chicken to do

anything. He'll get his."

"Hasn't there been enough getting?" Paul asked mildly.

Curtis gave him a quizzical look, then after a moment said, "Look you probably hate us for what we did. I guess we are just jealous of your background."

"Don't be, it's nothing to be jealous about," Paul said evenly. "I joined the army because my father wanted to dictate my life. He always gave me lectures about my station in life, about striving for higher stations, never look down. He insisted that if I must join the army I should either apply as an officer or a non-combatant, so I defied him and here I am. Who knows, maybe after the war, I'll go work as a miner or a lumberjack."

"You're probably stubborn enough to try," Curtis laughed as they continued to scrub the dishes. "I'll say something, you got guts and stamina. The sarge says that he could've transferred out if you would only rat on us, but you wouldn't."

"I would never do that," Paul said. "I may be a rich kid, but I'm not a squealer."

"No, you've got integrity and the Sarge shamed us all into realizing that, so here I am. I volunteered for kitchen duty and he accepted that as a confession."

"And the others followed you?"

"Yeah, but the sarge said there was no more room in the kitchen so he gave them latrine duty," Curtis laughed.

"Indeed, that is very interesting."

"I just want you to know, even though you will probably never call me a friend, we won't harass you any more," Curtis said with a great sigh.

"Do you speak for the others as well?"

"Yes, and if anyone ever calls you Rich Kid again, I'll punch *him* in the mouth."

They continued to dry dishes in silence for a-while, then

Curtis said, "I've been teasing you so long, I forgot your first name."

"It is Paul. Paul Cunningham."

"Alright, Paul Cunningham, I am Curtis Smith. How do you do?" Curtis extended his hand.

"Pleased to meet you, Curtis Smith," Paul said shaking his hand. "Shall we stand together as Canadian soldiers and make the Hun our enemy instead of each other?"

"It's a deal," Curtis smiled.

That evening when Paul and Curtis returned to their barracks the ever-vexatious Dale, who was standing beside his bunk, commented, "How do you like washing dishes with the rich kid?"

"Shut up, Runt," Curtis said pushing him hard enough that he fell down onto his bunk. "I didn't hear you volunteer for extra duty."

"Yeah, you weren't scrubbing any shitters," Bob said as he and Jim joined Curtis in forming a menacing semicircle around Dale's bunk.

"I wasn't an instigator," Dale said quickly with eyes darting around.

"But you were right in there, like one of those yappy little dogs," Bob replied.

Curtis then addressed his fellow squad members as a whole. "The rich kid is my friend and if anybody calls him that again, he'll have to answer to me. His name is Paul"

"He's my friend too," Bob added.

"And mine," Jim chimed in.

They all glowered at Dale.

"And as for the runt. . ," Curtis said, in a menacing tone.

Paul stepped into the semicircle, then addressed the squad, looking frequently at his new-found friends and Dale.

"There has been enough name calling and bad feeling. It is time to put all of this behind. I don't care if I am called rich kid, everyone has a nickname," then with a wry grin added, "even the runt."

The others all laughed.

Paul continued, "We are all Canadian soldiers. If we want to kick the Hun's ass, then we should all work together. The past is already forgotten in my mind and my fat lip is almost gone away."

Again there was laughter.

"Whaddya say Runt?" Paul laughed as he said to Dale, "wanna be buds with the rich kid?"

As all eyes were on him, Dale rose from his bunk and said with a smile of his own, "Sure Rich Kid." They clasped hands.

The sergeant who had been standing quietly at the far end of the tent said, "Well done, boys. Cunningham, Smith, Jones and White, you are henceforth relieved of KP duty."

"Yes sir," they replied in unison.

Paul now became friends with his former tormentors and they began to work together as a closely-knit team as they marched around the square or on long hikes over rugged snowbound terrain. If one, Paul in particular, faltered in any way, the others were there to look out for him, but he would always be called Rich Kid, however, only they were allowed to use that name.

Then one day training was over, they were all lined up again and told they were moving to a base near Toronto where they would be formed up into the North Ontario regiment. Upon arrival they were allotted five days of leave to visit their families before being shipped overseas.

Chapter Six

Paul walked smartly into the Toronto home of his father and was surprised to meet a petite olive-skinned girl in the main hallway, dressed in maid's attire. She was also startled at his abrupt appearance and said with a strong Italian accent, "Pardon *Signore*, do you belonga here?"

Paul chuckled and replied, "Yes, this is my father's house. And you must be. . ?"

"Gina, I ama the new maid."

"Paul," Ginny cried as she came into the hallway and rushed to embrace her brother. "You didn't tell us you were coming."

"We are finished training now and were given some leave to be with our families before going overseas," Paul smiled. "So we have a new maid now."

"Yes, Gina. We hired her two weeks ago." Turning to Gina, Ginny said with a smile, "Gina, this is my brother, Paul."

"We've met," Paul laughed.

"Do you want me to takea your bag?" Gina said in reference to the duffel bag Paul carried.

"Yes, please take it up to my room."

Gina took the large bag and struggled to take it up the stairs.

"Here, let me," Paul said as he bounded up beside her and took the bag.

"But I ama the maid," Gina protested.

"The bag seems heavy for you," Paul assured her.

As Paul came back down the stairs Ginny surveyed her brother, dressed smartly in his uniform. "My, you look handsome," she gasped. "Come," she said, grasping him by the hand. "Mother!" she cried as she tugged Paul along into the parlour. "Paul's home."

As they entered the parlour, Claire came into the room

from another direction.

"Paul," she cried as she rushed to embrace her son. "Good to see you home after the way you ran away on us."

"I'm sorry, but I had to do it that way to get past Father," Paul replied as he squeezed then let go of his mother. "How did he handle it?"

"He was shocked of course, but after he read the letter you wrote to Ginny, I think he respected your choice," Claire replied.

"Paul," another voice cried as Victoria ran up to him. Paul scooped up his thirteen-year-old sister hoisting her clear of the floor.

"How come you joined the army?" she asked.

"Well, our country is at war," he laughed.

"Daddy says that people of lower stations should do all the fighting."

"That's our Dad," Paul chuckled.

As they settled in the parlour, Gina brought in tea and snacks on a trolley.

"Thank you Gina," Claire said.

"I don't like those kind of cookies," Victoria complained upon seeing the cookies displayed on the tray.

"I'll bringa your favorites," Gina smiled.

"Oh Vicky, don't be so demanding," Ginny chided her.

"So, Ginny tells me Gina just started working here two weeks ago," Paul said, taking a cup of tea.

"Yes, she is still on a trial basis," Claire replied. "Robert has some concerns about her poor English.

"Yeah, I can't understand her," Victoria complained again.

"She speaks fairly clearly from what I have heard," Paul said.

"Yes, I am helping her with her English," Ginny said enthusiastically.

"My sister Ginny, always so full of compassion for others,"

Paul smiled.

Gina returned with some cookies of Victoria's liking and Victoria barely acknowledged Gina as she reached for one.

"You could at least say thank you," Ginny frowned at her.

"Why? She's just the maid."

"Your sister is right," Claire added. "One should always be polite even to the maid."

Victoria frowned, but said no more.

A short while later when Robert came home, they heard him speaking to Gina as she took his coat and hat. Paul stood up as Robert entered the parlour and Victoria rushed to hug him.

"Hello Father," Paul smiled.

"Hello son," Robert said evenly as he surveyed his son in uniform while he hugged his youngest daughter. "I have to admit, the uniform does something for you. I presume you have some leave."

"Yes, I have a week off, then we'll be forming a regiment and be going overseas."

"I see," Robert said as he let go of Victoria.

"That is if you wish me to be home," Paul added carefully.

"Well, I must say that I don't approve what you've done, but it's done now," Robert said frankly. "Yes, you are welcome to be at home. I can only hope that once you are through this foolishness, you will come back and find a respectable career."

"Yes, Father," Paul replied.

"Paul is only with us for a few days before he goes off to join that dreadful war," Claire said. "So let's not quarrel, but make the best of our time with him."

"Do we have a truce?" Paul said with a wry look.

"Yes, I will agree not to discuss your future during your stay with us," Robert grinned crookedly, extending his hand.

"Thank you, dear." Claire smiled broadly as the two men shook hands.

Gina appeared and offered a menu for dinner to supplement the meat course that Claire had requested earlier on. As usual, Victoria complained at the first selection, and Claire asked Paul to choose. Paul chose and Victoria complained again, but she was ignored by the others while Ginny commented on the excellent choice.

They dined at a table large enough to hold twenty. Robert was at the head, with Ginny and Paul on his left and Claire and Victoria on his right. As they ate, the subject of the war came up.

"It will be quite dangerous crossing the Atlantic with the submarines attacking the ships," Ginny ventured.

"Yes, well the ships travel in convoys now so it should be safe," Paul assured her.

"It was terrible how they sank the Lusitania, killing all those innocent civilians," Claire added. "Barbarians," Robert muttered. "No wonder they call the Germans the Hun."

"Is that in reference to Attila the Hun?" Ginny asked. "I learned in school how he was one of the most ferocious of the barbarians to sack the Roman Empire."

"Yes, that's it," Paul said. "It's called war propaganda. Just like they say German soldiers rape Belgian women and skewer children with their bayonets."

"Paul really," Claire said sharply. "Such talk in front of your sisters."

"I'm sorry, Mother, I guess being in the army has made me a little blunt," Paul replied.

"Germans have become so unpopular, that they renamed the city of Berlin, Ontario Kitchener," Robert added. "And the name of the royal family has been changed from the House of Hanover to the House of Windsor."

"Let's talk about something besides the war," Claire

suggested.

"All right, so what are your plans for next year, Ginny?" Paul asked.

"I guess I'll be going to finishing school," Ginny replied without enthusiasm.

"Finishing school will make a fine youg lady out of you," Claire said.

"I can hardly wait to go there," Victoria chimed in.

Ginny's eyes rolled upward and Paul smirked at her.

Sensing the interplay, Robert rumbled, "Finishing school will be good for you Ginny. Maybe it will get all these silly romantic notions out of your head and make you appreciate your station in life."

"Yes, Father," Ginny replied in a low voice.

Gina wheeled in a dessert trolley and distributed dishes of apple trifle around the table, then quickly left.

"Yum. It looks delicious," Paul remarked as he picked up his spoon.

"I'd rather have banana flavoured," Victoria complained.

"Why do you always complain about everything, Victoria?" Ginny chided her.

"I prefer to be called Vicky, Virginia," Victoria shot back.

"Enough, both of you," Robert rumbled.

As they finished dessert, Gina brought them tea, gathered up the dinner plates and serving bowels, then left again.

Robert took a sip of tea and turned to his son. "So Paul, what do you think of our new maid?"

"She seems to be quite efficient and is an excellent cook."

"Yes, that is true, but her language is a bit of a problem."

"I can understand her," Paul replied.

"And I'm teaching her better English in her spare time," Ginny said with enthusiasm.

"I don't know why you waste your time with her," Victoria added. "Can't we just hire a new maid who can speak English properly?"

"Victoria," Claire said sharply as Ginny scowled at her sister. "You are rude and inconsiderate. Gina is a good maid who does her job well and your sister is a very compassionate person for offering to help Gina with her English. Don't you think, Robert?"

"Uh, well yes," Robert replied. He had some reservations about Ginny being so concerned with the welfare of a mere maid. He would have dismissed Gina by now, because of her poor English, except for the pleading of both his wife and Ginny to keep her.

"Yes, Ginny has a heart of gold," Paul said, smiling at his sister. "She will no doubt be a great lady someday. I think it is very wonderful of her to have such compassion for someone who's only offense is that she is a newcomer to this land."

"Well said, Paul," Claire smiled.

Paul glanced at Ginny and she was smiling radiantly.

The following afternoon Paul took Ginny to an afternoon performance of the Toronto philharmonic symphony. Victoria was given the same offer, but declined because in her mind symphony was *too boring*. The program included a selection of lively Mozart pieces and the main feature was Beethoven's *Pastoral Symphony*.

"Thank you, Paul. That was beautiful," Ginny said as they left the concert hall. "*The Pastoral Symphony* has to be one of the most beautiful pieces of music I ever heard."

"Yes, it is very restful," Paul added.

"Just to listen to it creates a vision of travelling across the countryside on a beautiful summer day, complete with an afternoon thunderstorm." Ginny said dreamily as they walked along with her clutching her brother's arm.

"It's amazing how the Germans can create such beautiful

music and still make war," Paul remarked.

"These composers are mainly Austrian," Ginny replied. Then after a moment she sighed and added, "But we are at war with Austria also."

"Austrians and Germans are the same people," Paul said. "It's an accident of history that they are two different nations."

"You are so scholarly," Ginny smiled at her brother. Then changing the subject, she suddenly said, "Look there's a photo studio across the street. Let's go there. I'd like a picture of you in uniform before you go overseas and so, probably, would Mom and Dad.."

"Good idea," Paul replied. "I'd like one of you to take overseas also."

They crossed the street and quickly made their way to the studio.

"It's almost closing time," the proprietor said when they enquired about the photos.

"It should only take a few minutes to take a picture of both me and my sister," Paul persisted. "I will be going overseas within the week and it is important for my family to have a picture of me, and for me to have one of my sister."

The proprietor looked at his schedule and sighed. "There is one family in the studio now and since we have no more bookings, I suppose we can squeeze you in, providing you only want one pose each."

"One pose will do," Paul smiled.

"Is there a place where I can fix my hair?" Ginny asked.

"Yes, go down the hall to the first door on the right."

"Thank you."

While Ginny was attending to her hair, the family consisting of a man, woman and a youth about Paul's age with very light blond hair emerged from the studio. They were speaking to each other in a foreign language. When the man spoke to the proprietor in English, he had a curious accent that sounded as if he had a hot potato in his mouth.

The youth spoke to his father in English with the same hot-potato-in-the-mouth accent. "How will we get these pictures over to Denmark, Papa? The North Sea is blockaded."

"We'll find a way, Marty," the man replied. "We did get a letter from Martha since the war started."

"Do you want to do your photo first while your sister is getting ready?" the proprietor asked Paul.

"Sure," Paul smiled.

"Well, we'd better get going," the man said. "When will the photos be ready?"

"In a week's time."

"I don't have a week," Paul muttered. "I'll be heading overseas."

"You can develop the pictures for this gentleman first," the man said. "He is going to fight for our country."

The youth named Marty stole a look at Paul in uniform and Paul smiled back, then replied, "You are very kind, sir, but they can mail me my pictures. Army mail always gets through on time."

"I insist that you develop this soldier's pictures first," the man said. "I don't know when ours will get through to the Old Country anyway."

"Thank you, sir. . ."

"Jergen," the man smiled. "Good luck in fighting the Germans. They stole part of Denmark you know."

"Yes, Schleswig-Holstein." Paul laughed. "I studied history."

Both Jergen and Marty smiled at Paul as they turned to go out the door.

As the Danish family was leaving, Ginny emerged with her long hair neatly coifed.

"You look more beautiful than ever, dear sister," Paul smiled.

"And you are so handsome in your uniform."

"Shall we get on with the pictures," the proprietor said. "So we all can go home."

"Sorry for dawdling," Paul apologized.

As they went into the studio, Ginny asked. "Did you know those people who just left?"

"No," Paul replied. "They're from Denmark. Very nice people."

Paul returned to his barracks a few days hence. He and his tormentors turned friends were kept together in the same squad with a new sergeant. They were in turn made part of an infantry regiment. The regiment was subdivided into two battalions while they in turn were divided into four companies labelled after the first four letters of the alphabet. Paul was in C company. Each company was further subdivided into four platoons and they in turn were subdivided into four squads. On the other side, three regiments made up one brigade, and four brigades made up a division and four divisions made up a corps which was the sum total of the Canadian Army. The regiment was commanded by a colonel, the battalions by a lieutenant colonel, the companies by a captain, the platoons by a first lieutenant, and the squad by a sergeant. All units larger than a regiment were commanded by generals. Officers holding either the rank of second lieutenant or major had no specific command and were used for special assignment.

They were to be sent to Halifax by train before boarding a ship to England. Here they would undergo more training to be fully integrated into the greater British Army before heading for the front.

As they marched up to Union Station to board their train, their CO informed them that they would be allotted a few moments to say goodbye to their families. As Paul marched smartly along with his duffel bag and rifle over his shoulder, he saw his family waiting for him at the station

The company was then dismissed briefly so the soldiers could say goodbye to their loved ones. Paul approached them standing tall and proud in his uniform.

He approached his father first extending his hand. Robert clasped it and said, "All the best, son, may you find your destiny and come safely back to us."

"Thank you, Father," Paul replied, with the barest trace of emotion. "Who knows, when I get back I might even seek a respectable career."

They hugged each other momentarily before Paul spoke to his mother.

"Be careful over there," Claire said through teary eyes. "I won't sleep a wink while you are gone."

"I'll be back," Paul assured her. "I'll write to you often."

Paul and his mother hugged tightly for a long moment and she gave him a tear-soaked kiss on the cheek.

Paul then turned to Victoria and scooped her up into his arms. "Goodbye little sister; be a good girl while I'm gone."

"Goodbye Paul, will you send me a present from France?"

"I sure will," Paul assured her as he lowered her down.

He then turned to Ginny as if by unspoken understanding, they would be the last to say goodbye.

"Well goodbye Ginny," he said holding her with out-stretched arms. "Take good care of Mom and Dad, and little Vicky. I'll think of you when I'm away."

"I'll miss you, dear brother," Ginny sniffed. "I promise I'll write to you every day and promise me you'll return."

"I promise," Paul replied as he hugged Ginny tightly for a long moment. "I said I'd always be here for you."

The call came for the soldiers to form up and board the train

They all waved as they watched the troop train pull away on its way to Halifax. Paul waved at them one last time through the window.

Chapter Seven

When the train arrived at the bustling port of Halifax, Paul found it to be a collection area for soldiers from all over Canada. Two brigades, including a number of artillery batteries, were assembled for transport on two ships assigned for the task. Also included was the regiment from Newfoundland to be put on the same ship as Paul's regiment. Paul observed these curious people; many spoke with a lilt that sounded almost Irish in nature. These, almost Canadians, geographically part of Canada, but apart from Canada[1], had proudly formed their own regiment.

As the soldiers filed on board the ship, the vast enlisted ranks to which Paul belonged were placed in the lower sections. Far from the comfort that Paul remembered on the family voyage to England during his earlier youth, each soldier was assigned a hammock bed. These bag-like bunks were often stretched two and sometimes three tiers high. A small space was allotted to store his personal gear. The officers were accorded the upper decks.

As the ships escorted by two frigates from the Royal Navy set out across the cold grey Atlantic, Paul, like many others, felt the cold anxiety that they were heading for the war. There was also the concern that the German U-boats were laying in wait, although few ventured into the western Atlantic. During the crossing many of the soldiers played cards and gambled. Curtis and Dale watched their money ebb and flow several times during a marathon crap game held on the floor of their bunk area, while Bob White sat in on an ongoing poker game. Paul, who was

[1]Newfoundland did not become part of Canada until 1949 when it was accepted as the tenth province.

not prone to gambling, often wandered about or stood on deck looking out over the limitless ocean enjoying a cigarette from his new-found habit.

During one of his self-styled watches on the deck, he thought of that other time he had crossed the ocean and a curious incident that had occurred.

*　　　*　　　*

It was on the return voyage from England, Paul, Ginny and Victoria went for a stroll around the deck. They came to the front of the promenade where they could look down upon the bow.

"Let's go down to the bow," Ginny said eagerly. "I would like to look over the bow of the ship."

"Father said we shouldn't go down there," Victoria said. "All the lower class people are down there."

"Oh Father is always worrying about lower class people," Ginny scoffed. "You'd think they had some sort of disease or something."

"Father says they are all immigrants down below, that they stink and carry lice."

"Nonsense, Father sometimes makes a lot of to-do about nothing."

"Do you think that girl has lice?" Paul laughed as he pointed to a teenage girl who came out from below and sat on a bench by the railing. She had a magazine in her hand and began reading it.

"She looks harmless to me," Ginny said. "Let's go."

"I'm staying up here," Victoria said adamantly.

"You stay right here," Paul said. "Ginny and I will only be a moment as we just want to look over the bow of the ship."

Victoria watched as her brother and sister went

down the stairs, then ran to tell her parents that they had disobeyed instructions.

As they walked past the girl sitting on the bench, the girl looked up and smiled at Ginny. She was a very attractive girl with braided, golden-coloured hair.

Paul and Ginny continued along to the bow. Paul glanced back to the top of the stairs and remarked, "I don't see Vicky any more."

"She probably ran back to tell Mom and Dad that we went down to the bow," Ginny replied.

"Yes," Paul sighed. "We shouldn't stay down here too long, or we'll get a lecture from father about mingling with the immigrants."

"Yeah, Vicky is such a little tattle-tale." Ginny added. "I wonder where that girl sitting on the bench is from?"

"She's blonde, so she must be from northern Europe. Probably Scandinavian or Dutch," Paul replied, looking over the bow. "See how the ship is cutting the water."

Ginny also looked over the bow for a long moment observing how the ship was parting the water.

"We'd better get back," Paul said turning back from the bow.

"I suppose," Ginny sighed.

Just then a gust of wind came up and Ginny felt something against the back of her legs. It was the magazine belonging to the girl on the bench and the girl was scrambling after it. Ginny reached down and grabbed the magazine and smiled as she handed it back to the girl.

"Tank you much," the girl said in halting English as she took the magazine and went back to her bench.

As they returned from the bow, Ginny deliberately walked near the girl out of curiosity.

"Hello," the girl smiled.

"Hello," Ginny smiled sitting down beside her. Paul

grinned awkwardly. As a lad of awakening puberty, he thought the girl was extremely beautiful and she gave him butterflies in his stomach.

Glancing at the magazine the girl was reading and noticing the printing to be in a foreign language, Ginny asked, "Where are you from? That writing is different."

"I from Sveden, you not understand vords," the girl laughed.

"I'm from Toronto," Ginny said.

"Toronto in Canada, ya?"

"Are you going to Canada?"

"Go to Canada, ya," the girl said.

"We should get going, Ginny," Paul said anxiously as he saw his father at the top of the stairs.

"Is dat you name, Yinny?"

"Yes, my real name is Virginia, but everyone calls me Ginny."

"Yinny is nice name ya," the girl smiled.

"Let's get going," Paul said anxiously. "Father is coming."

"Paul and Ginny, come upstairs at once," Robert called from halfway down the stairs.

"Bye," Ginny said to the girl.

As they climbed back up the stairs toward their stern-faced father, Robert scolded them. "Now you two know better than to associate with people from the lower decks."

"Yes, Father," Ginny said with bowed head.

"Paul, you should especially know better," Robert continued as they all climbed back up to the promenade deck. "I don't want to see either of you down there again. Let's go join your mother and Victoria for tea."

As they approached the table where Claire and Victoria sat, Ginny scowled at her smug-looking little sister for tattling.

"I found these two down on the bow talking to some immigrant," Robert grumbled as they all sat at the table.

"Really, whatever possessed you two to go down there?" Claire said looking at Paul and Ginny.

"We wanted to look over the bow of the ship and see it split the water," Paul said innocently.

"You should have waited and asked me to escort you," Robert said. "You never know what sort of rabble is lurking in the steerage area of the ship."

"That girl didn't seem like rabble," Ginny said in a tone of defiance. "She was quite attractive, wasn't she Paul?" Ginny teased.

Paul blushed but made no comment.

"When I told her my name, she pronounced it, Yinny."

"Yinny, that sounds like a Norwegian or something," Claire remarked.

"She said she came from Sweden," Paul said abruptly.

"She probably has lice and fleas," Victoria chimed in.

"I don't think so," Ginny said sharply. "You should have come with us instead of being such a little snitch."

"Children, that will be enough," Claire admonished.

"Vicky did the right thing by coming to us," Robert added. "Like I said, I don't want you mingling with those people again."

"Why are we so much better than everyone else?" Ginny asked tearfully. "I was not allowed to be friends with Molly back at the estate, and that girl down on the deck seemed like a really nice person."

"Someday you will understand, dear," Claire said pleasantly as she sought to intercept another rant from Robert. "There is a purpose in the order of things and everyone has a place in it."

"Well said, dear," Robert replied.

Ginny sat with tears in her eyes for a long moment then rose from her chair and walked toward the railing to look down on the bow.

"She wouldn't dare go back down there, would she?" Robert rumbled.

"I'll go comfort her," Paul offered. "I promise I won't take her down there again."

"Thank you, dear," Claire replied.

When Paul came alongside Ginny, she was sobbing and looking down at the bow. The Swedish girl was still sitting on the bench, busy reading her magazine.

Paul put a consoling arm around Ginny and she turned to him, still sobbing, "It's so unfair. I hate being better than everyone else. Molly could have been a really good friend, and that Swedish girl down there, I would really like to talk to her. I've never met anyone from a foreign country before."

"I know," Paul said. "Father is so worried that we will be contaminated or something."

"I'll bet that girl and her family are among those brave pioneers heading for the new western provinces." Ginny said.

"Probably. They say a lot of Swedish people are heading west, especially to the bush land," Paul continued in a gentle voice.

"When I grow up, I want to be in a world where all people are the same with no snobs looking down on the poor people."

"Yes, I've thought of that also," Paul replied. "But for now we must obey Father as we are still a long ways from growing up."

"I suppose you are right." Ginny smiled weakly at him.

"Come Ginny, let's go stroll around the promenade. Maybe we should go upstairs where the really rich people are. I don't think Father would complain about that."

Ginny laughed and clasped her brother's hand. "I'll follow you and there'll be no looking down."

*   *   *

Paul came back to the present reality as one of the Newfoundlanders, puffing on a small crooked pipe in his mouth, came up to Paul.

"Tis a cold miserable day," he said with his curious accent that sounded as if his mouth was full. "Watchin' fer de U-boats are ye?"

"Yeah, there's not much else to do besides gamble away your pay."

"Yeah, dere is dat. Good fishin' weather it is."

"Yes, I guess you do a lot of fishing in Newfoundland," Paul said with a friendly smile.

"Yeah, dere is not much else to do on de Rock," he replied. "So, where are ye from?"

"Toronto," Paul replied. "And where in Newfoundland are you from?"

"Corner Brook"

"So, I suppose you are a fisherman?" Paul continued.

"Yeah, bin on the boats since I was fourteen. We fish in the Gulf, we do," he said in reference to the Gulf of St. Lawrence. "You sound like an educated man."

"Well I started to go to university, but I quit and joined the Army," Paul laughed.

"Yeah, a lot a young men quit de boats to join de army. Us Newfies formed our own regiment to fight the Hun, we did," he said with much pride.

"Your own island having its own regiment; that is

something to be proud of," Paul replied.

"Yeah, dey lumped us in wit de British Army, but we'd ruther be wit de Canadians."

"Even our so-called Canadian Army is still under the overall command of the British." Paul chuckled. "Anyway, Newfoundland is almost part of Canada."

"Some say we should join Canada, others say we should be on our own."

"What do you say?"

"I think we should join. We're too per to be on our own."

"You're probably right," Paul replied. "By the way, my name is Paul Cunningham."

"Please to meet ye, my name is Tom Brady," Tom replied as they shook hands.

"It's getting chilly out here," Paul said with a shiver. "I think I'll go below."

"Come wit me to where our b'ys are," Tom offered. "We'll treat ye to music and beer."

"Thanks, that sounds like fun."

As they entered the area of the ship where the Newfoundland regiment was quartered, Paul could hear lively fiddle music that was clearly Celtic in nature. It consisted of a lone fiddler, a corporal by his stripes. Several others were clapping to the beat.

"Get us a couple a beers Alex," Tom said to one of his fellow soldiers, "We have a guest."

"Who might de guest be?" Alex asked when he returned with two mugs of beer.

"Tis Paul Cunningham from Toronto," Tom replied. To Paul he said, "This is me bud, Alex McDonough. He looks after de beer. Us Newfies make our own kind of beer, we do."

"It's good beer too," Paul replied, savouring the

frothy drink. "Who is your fiddler?"

"Tis Robbie Murphy. He's the best fiddler in our outfit, he is." Tom replied.

"It's good music," Paul said as took another sip of the Newfoundland beer.

"Yer from Toronto ye say," Alex said with a friendly grin. "Me father was in Toronto once. He says it is very big city."

"It is. It is the second largest in Canada," Paul laughed. "Are you from Corner Brook also?"

"No, I'm from a village near St. Johns. Tom and I became buds when we joined up, we did. So what brings a man from Toronto down to visit wit the squid-jiggers?"

"Tom invited me and I find your whole setting here quite charming."

"Charming is it. Ye sound like one of them upper class college b'ys," Alex frowned.

"I started university, but I'm not upper class," Paul smiled. "I quit so I could fight for my country, just like you."

"We got our own regiment," Alex said with much pride. "We're goin' over dere, to give de Hun a good fight."

"So I heard," Paul smiled. "Even though I'm from Toronto, I got put in the North Ontario regiment. It includes men from all over. My best friend, Curtis, is from Winnipeg, Manitoba."

"When we git over dere, dey'll make us part a de British Army," Tom added.

"Yeah, they don't think Canada is a country on its own yet," Paul sighed.

"And Newfoundland is just per relations," Tom laughed. "Dey tink us notting but fishermen."

"Ah, but us herring chokers 'll show de Hun a ting or two." Alex added.

"I'm sure you will," Paul chuckled.

On the sixth day out, the convoy was joined by two more Royal Navy destroyers. As they were now approaching the territorial waters of the British Isles, there was sure to be U-boats lurking nearby. Forty-eight hours later they safely arrived at Portsmouth and Paul posted letters to both his mother and Ginny. From Portsmouth they marched several miles inland to a major base camp for a few weeks of additional training before going to the front.

Chapter Eight

On the first morning on parade, they were lined up in platoon-sized batches for inspection in full gear, while a scowling sergeant major paced up and down slapping a baton against his hand. Their own squad leaders as staff sergeants, were one rank below him, also stood in rigid anticipation. He stepped back a few paces and finally barked at them with his sharp English accent.

"For this training I am your commander and it is my job to make soldiers out of you colonial rabble."

"We are not colonials, we are Canadians," Bob said in a low voice to Curtis who stood rigidly beside him.

"What was that, soldier?" the sergeant barked as he stepped up to the now trembling Bob.

"We are Canadians, sir," Bob said in a small voice.

"I don't care if you are Canadians, Australians, or South African Bushmen, you are all colonials and I mean to bring you up to British Army standards," he shouted in Bob's face. "Is that clear, soldier?"

"Yes, sir," Bob replied with a weak voice.

"And you, soldier," he said to Curtis, who was frozen at attention. "Did you shave this morning?"

"Yes, sir."

"I can see a few whiskers," the sergeant continued relentlessly.

"Yes, sir. I will do better tomorrow morning, sir."

"As a reminder, you will step out of line and make two laps around the parade square," the sergeant barked. "On the double!"

Curtis stepped out of line and quickly jogged around the perimeter of the square.

The sergeant paced for a few moments then stopped

at Paul. "Soldier, the puttee on your left leg is crooked.

"Yes, sir," Paul said smartly. "Permission to fix it, sir."

"Permission granted," the sergeant replied. "Be on the double. Oh, and while you are down there do ten push-ups."

Paul knelt down and quickly attended the task, while Dale let out a tiny snicker. After all this time Paul still could not seem to do up his puttees to satisfy a sergeant.

"Is something funny, soldier!" the sergeant barked.

"No, sir," Dale replied as his face froze in an expressionless mode.

"Take one step forward, soldier," the sergeant continued.

Dale promptly obeyed and the sergeant eyed him over, picking at his uniform, complaining that his buttons and shoes weren't polished well enough. He took Dale's rifle, looked it over, threw it back at Dale and said,"You call that a well-kept rifle, hah! You, also, two laps around the square."

As the sergeant major made his way up and down the line, he soon had a dozen soldiers either doing push-ups or jogs around the square for minor infractions that displeased him. Attention was rapt and rigid as the ranks stood frozen in their tracks, fearful of what the sergeant major might find next.

When all the various soldiers called out were back in line, the sergeant paced and addressed the whole platoon. "Because you are colonial rabble, certain minor infractions have been tolerated this morning, but from now on sloppiness of uniform and whiskers will not be tolerated. When you go to the front, you will be facing the mightiest and most ferocious army the world has ever seen. The Hun lives and breathes military discipline. The Prussian nation which is at the heart of this so-called German Empire is a military machine that thrives on war. This is an army that is fighting the Russian, French and British armies all at the same time. An army that has our French allies against the wall at Verdun as we speak. If we are to beat this army, we must be better than this army, and the core of any good army is discipline."

"Yes, sir," they all shouted in unison.

"About face," the sergeant shouted and the soldiers all turned as one unit.

"Quick march!" he bellowed

As they marched around the parade square stopping, starting and turning according to the sergeant's whim, Paul could hear the strains of a popular tune in his head. *'It's a long way to Tipperary, it's a long, long way to go.'* Its martial beat was in tune with the rigid parade step.

For the next six weeks they drilled relentlessly, both on the parade square and across country. They sprang out of trenches, they learned how to leap over barbed wire or crawl under it. They skewered straw dummies dressed in German uniforms with their bayonets, crying, "Kill the Hun, kill the Hun!" They were exposed to live fire with both machine-guns and artillery fired over top of them as they lay hugging the ground.

Finally at the end of this exhaustive training, they were accorded some leave. At the end of this leave they would be sent to France for a brief final preparation for the front at a base camp near Etaples.

The day his outfit was granted leave, Paul received a note delivered by courier from Sir Wilfred Crawley. It was an invitation to come to his estate to spend his leave.

"So, what have you got there?" Curtis asked as he saw Paul reading the note.

"A note from Sir Wilfred to come to his estate," Paul replied blandly.

"I might have guessed! The rich kid gets to go to some fancy estate," Curtis laughed. "Too good to come downtown with the rest of us lower class rabble."

"Speaking of Rich Kid, if you saw this guy's place you'd think that I lived in poverty," Paul said with a grin. "It's a family thing, probably arranged by my father. I doubt if I'll be there long. Approximately where about in London are the boys going?"

"Probably around Piccadilly. They say there is lots of entertainment around there."

"Good. If I should get bored staying in those lofty heights, I'll know where to find you guys."

"You'd better not stay too long, we only have three days off before going to the front."

"Yeah, I hope I can find you guys."

"Just check out the pubs and brothels around there, you'll find us. Just don't get too stuffed on caviar and champagne."

Paul arrived at the estate. As Charles answered the door, he studied the young man in uniform for a moment, then said finally, "Master Paul?"

"Yes. Paul Cunningham. Sir Wilfred sent for me."

"Yes, he did say you were coming. Come right in. Master Jonathan is home also on leave."

"Perhaps we can go riding again," Paul said with a smile as he entered the big house.

As they entered the main hall, Sir Wilfred was there to greet him. He had aged noticeably in the six years since the Cunningham family were his guests.

"Paul, it is good that you could come," he clasped Paul's hand, and surveyed his uniform. Then looking at him quizzically, asked, "Where are your decals? Your uniform looks rather plain."

"Decals?" Paul replied. Then presuming that Sir Wilfred expected him to be an officer, he replied. "I'm in the enlisted ranks."

"You don't say. I thought your father would have gotten you a commission."

"He wanted me to be an officer, but if I am to fight for my country I want to be in the thick of things."

"I say, you Canadians have no sense of class. None-theless you did volunteer to serve the Empire to stop the Hun, so you are welcome in my house. Come to the drawing room. If you are old enough to go to war, you're old enough to have a man's drink."

When they entered the drawing room, Jonathan, who had been sitting rose to greet them.
"Jonathan," Paul beamed. He failed to notice that Jonathan was in an officers uniform. He had been thinking of the youth who treated him kindly many years before. "You've joined up also."

He coldly looked over Paul's uniform and replied, "Are you not an officer, soldier?"

"No, I joined the enlisted ranks."

"Did they not teach you any proper respect in the Canadian Army?" Jonathan said in a commanding tone of voice.

"Yes sir! Sorry sir!" Paul came to attention and snapped a salute.

"Better. Then turning to Sir Wilfred, talking as if Paul wasn't there, he continued, "Father, why have you invited a mere private to our home?"

"I invited Paul, son of my Canadian associate, Robert Cunningham. You surely remember him from that time the Cunningham family was here. I was also surprised that he was not an officer also, but he is a guest nonetheless."

"In the army, we were taught not to associate with the enlisted ranks," Jonathan continued. Turning to Paul he continued, "I am Lieutenant Crawley to you."

"Yes sir," Paul replied in a small voice.

"I'm afraid my son takes his rank rather seriously," Sir Wilfred interjected. "But surely in our own house we can relax a little."

"You may stay as it is my father's wish, but I cannot associate with you on a personal level. Whatever you remember of your earlier time at this house must be forgotten in the present situation."

"I understand, sir," Paul replied. "I guess there'll be no horseback riding."

"I'm afraid not, soldier," Jonathan continued. "Some of my fellow officers are coming tomorrow to go riding and it would not do to have a mere private along."

"No sir, it wouldn't," Paul replied. "Perhaps I should take my leave and go back to London."

"Nonsense," Sir Wilfred replied. "It is getting late and I insist that you have dinner and at least one overnight stay with us. That is if Jonathan doesn't mind sitting at the same table as us."

Jonathan drew a breath and said, "I can concede this time, but Father and you, Paul, must understand that discipline and rank structure are crucial to any army. Why do you think the German Army is so powerful? Every soldier and officer knows his place and follows the order of command to the letter. If we are to beat the Hun, our army has to at the very least, meet their standards."

"Yes sir," Paul replied. "My drill sergeant said much the same thing, sir."

"He was right you know."

"Of course, sir. I'll be leaving in the morning, hopefully before your fellow officers get here, sir."

"Now that all is said and done, can we relax as people

for the rest of the evening.?" Sir Wilfred declared. "After all, you are both serving His Majesty and are about to go forth and help our French allies turn back the Hun."

Paul looked to Jonathan and Jonathan slowly replied, "You're at ease for the duration, soldier. Or should I say Paul. I ask only that you address me as Lieutenant and you may forgo the requirement that you salute me while in this house."

"Yes Lieutenant," Paul replied.

Sir Wilfred poured Paul a drink of strong whiskey for which he was more than ready.

Dinner was somewhat more relaxed and Jonathan even asked Paul a few questions of the Canadian Army. Nonetheless, Paul felt decidedly out of place. The following morning when he came down for breakfast, he found the dining room occupied with Jonathan and several of his officer friends. He stopped short of going into the dining room knowing his presence would not be welcome.

"Master Paul," Charles said, coming along side him. "Sir Wilfred has asked you to join him for breakfast in the drawing-room."

When Paul entered the drawing-room after quickly stepping past the doorway into the dining room, Wilfred was sitting at a small table with breakfast served.

"Come sit down, Paul," he smiled. "I didn't want to sit with a bunch of rowdy officers either."

Paul smiled with no comment as he sat down. Then, as his breakfast plate was brought to him, he asked, "Could I trouble your chauffeur to drive me to the train station as soon as I've had breakfast?"

"That anxious to leave are you?"

"It's just, that if I stay here, I'll be spending all my time saluting and standing at attention."

"I see your point," Wilfred chuckled. "It shall be arranged."

As Paul rode the train back to London, he was glad to get back to Curtis and the boys. Although he was sure they would continue to call him Rich Kid, he knew he was much closer to them than he could ever be to Jonathan, a real rich kid.

Paul spent most of the day looking around the historic sights of London and when evening approached, he headed for that area of London around Piccadilly where his friends said they would likely be. There was at least a chance, in this vast city of millions, that he might run across some of the boys. The area abounded with pubs, brothels and floor shows where singers and actors performed, while the streets were full of off-duty servicemen. Paul strolled down the street past several pubs from which issued noisy laughter and singing. Then he came to one where he heard lively Celtic-flavoured fiddle music. He thought of Tom Brady and the other Newfoundlanders.

As he entered the pub, sure enough it was filled with the boys from the Royal Newfoundland regiment. Two fiddlers were performing while others sang, clapped and swilled beer. Some of them had women on their knees or in their arms as they listened.

"Paul b'y," called a familiar voice. "Came into town did ye?"

Paul turned and said, "Hi Tom, I thought it was you guys when I heard the music."

"Yeah, we're givin' de English ladies a bit a our entertainment," Tom grinned. "Can I get ye a pint? It's not like good Newfie beer, but it'll do."

"Thank you," Paul grinned as Tom motioned to the bartender.

"Did you not get yerself a bit of fluff ta keep ye company befer we go to de front?" Tom chuckled.

"Not yet," Paul smiled shyly. "I just got into town and am looking around."

"Time's a wastin' is it not?" Tom chuckled. "Take like Sadie here," Tom continued as he put his arm around an overly-dressed heavily-perfumed woman sitting on a bar stool beside him. Her face and hair both had artificial colouring..

She turned and said, with a smile in a sharp Cockney accent, "Awe Tom, what you got 'ere." She looked over the youthful, shyly smiling Paul. "Another of yer 'erring chokers. 'E still looks wet behind the ears 'e does."

She let out a burst of coarse laughter that made Paul uncomfortable. He took a swallow of the watery wartime beer.

"He's a real Canadian, from Toronto," Tom chuckled.

"A real Canydian, blimey, I thought you Newfies was Canydians."

"Well, er almost. Newfoundland should be part a Canada," Tom replied.

"Maybe one day you will be," Paul added.

"Do real Canydians fiddle like this too?" Sadie asked.

"Sometimes," Paul chuckled. "The French-Canadians are good fiddlers."

"Yeah, I heard some Acadians fiddle once," Tom said, "They can fiddle almost as good as us Newfies. Say Sadie, can ye find a lady fer Paul?"

"There's lots a lydies about that will keep company with a rich Canydian bloke."

"I'm not rich," Paul said through gritted teeth.

"Gaw on all Canydians are rich," she laughed.

"Not this Canadian. Thanks for the offer anyway, I should push on and see the sights in this part of London." He quaffed the remainder of his beer.

"Stay and we'll fix ye up wit a bit of fluff," Tom said. "Ye know times a wastin', we got only to tomorrow noon to get back to base. Den it's off to de front."

"When you see all the sights, come on back. Maybe we can find you a lydy." Sadie added with her coarse laugh. "One or two bob can get a quick fix."

Paul looked perplexed.

"A bob is a shilling," Tom said in reference to the British coin.

"When I get tired of looking around, I'll come back," Paul replied.

"Don't lose yer way now," Tom smiled as Paul moved toward the door.

"I'll listen for the music," Paul laughed. "Newfoundland music has a style of its own."

Paul continued down the street for another couple of blocks until another familiar voice called out, "Hey Rich Kid, what are you doing out this late at night?"

Paul turned to find Curtis grinning at him. He also had an arm around an overly-dressed and heavily-made-up woman and he seemed a little unsteady on his feet.

'This place must abound in prostitutes,' Paul thought.

"I wondered if I might find some of you guys," Paul smiled. "I just came from the pub where all the Newfies are holed up. Good fiddle music."

"Wanna go hear some fiddle music, Maggie?" Curtis asked in a slurred voice.

"Fiddle music! I 'ate fiddle music," Maggie replied. She had the same sharp Cockney accent as Sadie.

"This is good fiddle music. It's Newfie music."

"What the blazes is Newfie music?"

"From Newfoundland. An island full of fishermen from over by Canada."

"The only fishermen I've seen are the fishmongers down at the wharfs. They don't look like fiddlers. Besides, ya didn't py me Madam a quid to listen to fiddle music did you?"

"A quid?" Paul asked.

"Yeah, a one pound note," Curtis grinned sheepishly. "That's the going rate for an overnight lady."

"Don't ferget the pack a fags," Maggie said.

"Oh yeah, you gotta throw in a pack of cigarettes as well," Tom added.

"The one Tom Brady had said you could get a quick fix for a shilling," Paul replied.

"A bob for a quick fix, that's a bloody gull. But then you Canydians are all rich anyway."

"So why don't you get yourself a lady for the night?" Curtis asked. "It is getting late and you'll need to sleep somewhere."

"I only have two pound and a sixpence left to my name."

"So, tonight is our last night out before we go to the front. We may never come back you know."

"I will," Paul said confidently. "I made a promise to my sister."

"E made a promise to his sister," Maggie mocked. "Well, ain't that nice!"

"Well, I should be going," Paul replied growing irritated by the woman. "I'll look around for a while before deciding how I'll spend my night."

"Well hurry up old buddy," Curtis slurred. "The good ones are going fast."

'Well. If Maggie and Sadie are the good ones. . ,' Paul thought as he turned to walk away.

"See ya later," Curtis slurred, "Remember who I said was a soldier's best friend."

Chapter Nine

On the next block Paul came to an entertainment hall offering a singing group and featuring a female vocalist named Chelsea Pickford. He studied the features of the vocalist as depicted on the large colour poster with her long tumble-down, loose auburn ringlets, combed close around her heart-shaped face.

'Beautiful,' he thought. *'She's beautiful.'*

He entered the building and said to the ticket collector, "How much to get in?"

"Eh what, the show's 'alf over," the ticket man replied.

"Will Chelsea be on again?" Paul said anxiously.

"I should sy so, she's the myn attraction."

"How much to get in then?"

"A sixpence and a ha-penny."

"I got a sixpence, but you'll have to break a pound note for the ha-penny."

"Just give me the ruddy sixpence, since you missed 'alf the bloomin' show anyway."

Paul flipped out the coin on to the counter and was admitted. He made his way through the darkened sitting area as a troupe was singing and marching around on stage singing a popular tune called *A Long, Long Trail a Winding.* and found a seat about half way toward the front. Most of the other patrons were soldiers though many had female companions.

When the troupe had finished the number and the applause had died down, the emcee announced that Chelsea was coming on stage. She strode confidently on to centre stage amid whistles and cheering, far more beautiful than any poster could depict. Paul was captivated

In a clear voice she announced that she was going to sing an old English ballad, and thus began to sing *Barbara Allen* in a rich tremulous voice with piano accompaniment.

When the song ended there was an outburst of applause and cheering. Paul cheered more than anyone. Her second song, an enchanting ballad named *Wally Wally*, was too much. Although he was no doubt just another faceless entity in the audience, Paul felt as though she was looking directly at him' singing only for him. Paul got up and moved to the front row. He stood as there were no seats available. Other patrons shouted at him to get out of the way. He then squatted down in the aisle.

'My God, she's beautiful and she sings like an angel,' Paul thought. *'I must meet her.'*

When this number was over, she said goodnight to the audience in a soft clear voice and strode off stage disappearing behind the curtains amid wild cheering and whistling. Paul got up and sought a side entrance to the backstage area as another entertainer came on stage. He found a side door and entered. As he came to an area abounding in cubicles where the entertainers prepared themselves, a large man with a deep frown stepped in his way.

"What are you doing back here, soldier?" he demanded. "Patrons are not allowed backstage."

"I would like to speak to Chelsea, if just for a moment," Paul pled as the man physically blocked his path.

"Do you know how many ruddy soldiers try to get back here to see Miss Pickford? Now get out before I throw you out.".

"No doubt, lots," Paul replied as he tried to look around the large man.

"Eh now, don't get cheeky with me, young man."

Just then Chelsea emerged from a side doorway and looked their way. She smiled at the star-crossed young soldier trying to peer around the bouncer.

"Chelsea!" Paul cried. "Could I speak to you for a moment?"

"That's it, out you go," the bouncer said gruffly as he grabbed Paul by the shoulder of his tunic .and began to shove him toward the door.

"You're a beautiful singer," Paul gasped as he was being handled. "Can I get an autographed picture?"

Paul was marched through the main hall amid mirthful faces and ejected from the premises.

"Don't let him in here again," the bouncer said to the ticket man.

As Paul looked back, the ticket collector shook his head. "You soldiers never learn. You can't just go back into the entertainer area."

Paul started down the street with the vague idea that he might as well go join the Newfoundlanders for a good party when the angelic vision of Chelsea crossed his mind.He simply must meet her. He went back around behind the entertainment hall to look for a backdoor. Upon finding it, he discovered that it was locked from the inside, no doubt to keep intruders like himself out. He decided to wait around for her to come out as the show should be over soon. He sat down on a crate and lit a cigarette.

In a while there was a commotion inside and the backdoor opened. Paul quickly stepped into the shadows on the other side of the narrow street lest that bouncer appear. The singing troupe all filed out and turned out of the alley to head down the street chattering among themselves as they went. Then as a cab pulled up, Chelsea stepped out and Paul felt his heart in his throat. The bouncer appeared in the doorway, no doubt to make sure Chelsea got safely into the cab. From his place in the shadows Paul slipped up beside the taxi. As Chelsea climbed into the cab, the bouncer went back inside, assuming all was well. Paul quickly opened the other door and climbed in beside Chelsea. She let out a small startled cry and Paul said with a grin, "Mind if we share, Miss Chelsea? I'll pay the tab."

"I say, you are impertinent are you not," she said in an

annoyed tone.

"I just wanted to have a few words with you. I am just a lonely soldier far from home." Paul smiled with pleading eyes.

The cab remained stationary and the driver who had seen Paul's impromptu entry came around to see if all was well.

"I say young man," he frowned at Paul, "this cab is reserved for Miss Chelsea here. If you don't get out, I'll drive straight to the police station."

Paul gave Chelsea his best pleading look and her heart began to melt.

"It's all right driver, we'll share," Chelsea assured him.

"We're old friends who haven't seen each other in a while," Paul added.

"It's your decision, Miss Chelsea, I'll throw the blighter out if you wish."

"Carry on, I assure you it will be all right."

"As you wish. Just give a yell at the first sign of trouble."

As the cabby got back into his seat, Chelsea said with a scoff, "Old friends indeed, I don't even know your ruddy name."

"Paul, my name is Paul Cunningham. I am with the North Ontario regiment."

"I thought you might be a Canadian by the way you talk," Chelsea replied while looking ahead.

"And you, by the way you talk, you're not from London are you?"

"I'm from Kent, my father is a postmaster and he also has a small orchard just outside of Dover."

Upon hearing the name Dover, Paul couldn't resist singing a line from an old song, *"We will drive through fields of clover to the cliffs of Dover on our Golden Wedding day."*

Caught in the lighthearted mood that Paul generated,

Chelsea began to sing another line of the song, *"put on your old grey bonnet with the blue ribbon on it,"* then abruptly stopped and turned to Paul with a frown. "So what did you wish to talk to me about? Or do you think me a trollop you can get for a cheap trick?"

"Heavens no," Paul said with a start. "If it was a cheap trick I was after, I could get plenty of that on the street."

"You try to get past the bouncer to speak to me, and you lay lurking in the shadows so you can jump in the cab beside me. What is it that you want?"

"I want to get to know you," Paul said innocently. He looked directly at her and said, "You're so beautiful, and your singing is positively angelic. I was hypnotized."

"That's a new line," she laughed. "Are all you Canadians so familiar?"

"Have other Canadians tried to approach you?"

"A few soldiers have tried to get backstage, but you're the first to jump into a cab with me."

"I must apologize for being so forward, but I just had to meet you. You see it is my last night before going to the front." Paul stopped and added soberly, "You've probably heard that line before also."

"Not directly, but it is a line that a soldier would use." Chelsea smiled coyly. "You have such innocent eyes for someone who is so ruddy brazen. Where in Canada are you from?"

"I'm from Toronto. It is Canada's second largest city.

Chelsea was silent and they rode along in silence for a few moments until Paul asked, "How did you come to be an entertainer?"

"Well, everyone said I have a nice voice."

"That's an understatement," Paul interrupted.

"So, after the war started, they were looking for singers to entertain the troops." Chelsea continued, "Chas who is my boss was in Dover and heard me sing at a local pub. So he offered me a job in his company."

"He was a wise man." Paul said as the cab stopped outside an apartment building.

"Oh blimey, we're already at my flat," Chelsea said, disappointed that they had arrived so soon.

"May I be so bold as to ask if you would write to me?" Paul asked, giving her that pleading look again.

"There goes that look again. I say, do you do this to all the ladies?"

"Only to very special ones with beautiful voices."

"Well, all right, what's your address?" Chelsea sighed.

Paul rattled off the address of his regiment.

"Do you expect me to remember all that?"

"What's yours? I'll write first."

Chelsea rattled off her address.

Paul laughed and said, "Do you expect me to remember all that?" mimicking her statement. "You don't have a pencil do you?"

"No. I have a pen in my flat though."

The cabby came and opened the door.

"I'll run in and jot down my address," Chelsea said over her shoulder as the cabby helped her out. Paul followed.

As Chelsea went up the steps of her apartment, Paul turned to the cabby and handed him a one pound note.

"The fare is only half a crown. Or shall I wait, sir?"

"No, go on" Paul said wryly. "I'll catch another cab later."

"I'll get your change directly."

"No, keep the change. It's for looking after Chelsea so well."

"Thank you, sir," the cabby said as he climbed back into his seat.

Paul smiled as he watched the cab pull away, then Chelsea appeared with a note in her hand.

"Did you let the cab go?' she asked suspiciously.

"Yes," Paul smiled. "There are plenty of other cabs to catch, besides we haven't finished our conversation yet."

"Haven't finished?" Chelsea said with a frown. "Are you so presumptions as to think that I will invite you into my flat? What incredible cheek you Canadians have."

Paul looked up at the warm summer night, drew a deep breath and replied with his melting smile, "It's a nice night out, perhaps we could go for a walk."

"Go for a walk! You're off your chump. Do you have any idea what time it is?"

"It's a little late, but I've got 'till noon tomorrow to report to my outfit." Paul grinned at her.

"Well, I don't really feel like a walk. I would invite you in for a cup of tea, but my neighbours might think me a tart for inviting a gentleman in this time of night."

"They appear to all be in bed," Paul said observing the darkened houses around him.

"You have all the answers, don't you?" she said with a crooked grin. "If I let you in, you must promise not to take advantage of me."

"Absolutely," Paul grinned. "I wouldn't want to ruin a perfectly good relationship, at least until you give me that slip of paper with your address."

"I say, there is no end to you," she smiled crookedly as she clutched the paper tightly to her bosom, "I shall hang onto it to the end. Come, lets go in before one my neighbours awakens."

They entered her small apartment. It was dimly lit with a small electric light. Paul watched her light a few candles, then switch off the electric light. "We have to save on current as part of the war effort," was her only comment.

She pulled out the small tank from a portable stove and shook it saying, "There should be enough paraffin to boil a pot of tea, bloody wartime rationing!"

"I wouldn't want you to burn up any of the fuel for my sake."

"It's all right, I would have made a spot of tea before retiring anyway," Chelsea said as she lit the stove. "I hope you won't mind some old tea mixed with the new. The way those bloody submarines are trying to starve us to death, we can't even get in a decent amount of tea in. Are things this bad over in Canada?"

"No, there is plenty of everything over there. Not many of the U-boats get over to our side of the ocean."

"They say Canada is a vast land."

"Only Russia is larger," Paul replied.

They sat by candlelight over a cup of tea and biscuits and talked of many things with conversation running well past the last drop of tea being poured. Then during a lull in the conversation, Chelsea glanced at the clock on the wall. "Good God. It's 2 AM!"

"Oh my gosh, I should get out of here," Paul said, rising from the sofa.

"There'll likely be no cabs this time of night," Chelsea said, moving toward the door with him.

"Then I shall have to walk." Paul had one hand on the doorknob, but made no effort to turn it.

"Where will you stay? Everything will be closed," Chelsea said in an anxious tone.

Her hand brushed against Paul's and he grasped it, drawing her near to him as he bent her arm behind her back. She looked dreamily up at him and said, "Are you taking advantage of me?"

"I wouldn't think of it," Paul replied softly as they turned to each other and their lips met.

They kissed for a long moment and Paul said with his cheek on hers, "If I may be so presumptuous. . ."

"You've been quite presumptuous so far this evening,"

Chelsea cooed.

"I think I love you."

"Oh go on," she taunted as she drew back though still holding him at arm's length. "How old are you?"

"Nineteen. Does one have to be a certain age to know love?"

"A lonely soldier far from home, you hear me sing and think you are in love."

"I am in love," Paul said with his pleading eyes. "You must have some feeling for me or you would have thrown me out by now."

"It's those ruddy eyes of yours, I bet you've had lots of ladies running after you."

"No. I'm usually shy around women."

"You could have fooled me," Chelsea scoffed.

"Please still promise to write to me?"

"Oh, Paul," Chelsea sighed as she hugged him tightly and buried her face in his tunic. "You have me all confused. Yes, I promise to write to you."

"If you give me that note with your address, I'll be on my way," Paul said letting go of her.

She handed him the note and he stuffed it in his tunic pocket. As he turned to go, she caught him by the hand again. "You might as well stay the night. You can sleep on the sofa."

"Thank you," Paul breathed.

"I'll fetch you a blanket."

As she brought him the blanket she said with a wry grin, "I warn you not to get any ideas though, I keep a poker at my bedside in case of burglars."

"If I had any ideas, I would have stayed downtown where overnight ladies can be had for a pound, or quid as they call it."

"Oh take this and get some sleep," she scoffed as she threw the blanket at him. Without another word, Chelsea went through to the bedroom.

Paul settled down for the night on the sofa with a stomach full of butterflies as he thought of Chelsea. Sometime later he woke with a start. Chelsea was standing beside the sofa looking at him. She seemed like an angel in her white gown. Paul reached up for her and she grasped his hand. She gave a gentle tug and Paul rose from the sofa as if he were a featherweight and he seemed to glide on air as she led him through to her bedroom.

Later as she lay in his arms, he was convinced that she must be an angel, for he was in paradise.

Paul was the first to awaken. Chelsea's head was still resting on his chest and he gently stroked her long hair causing her to murmur. She slowly came awake and looked up at him and smiled.

"Good morning," Paul smiled back. "You look beautiful in the morning."

"I can't believe what I have done," she said with a curious grin. "A total stranger jumps into my cab, throws himself at me like a ruddy lovesick puppy, and I invite him into my bed. It's positively unheard of. Why, I've never done this thing before."

"Am I the first man in your life?"

"I've had one or two gentlemen knock me up, but that only after I've been acquainted with them for a while. I've certainly never had any of them stay overnight, especially in my bed."

"Knock you up you say?" Paul chuckled.

"Yes. Why is that so funny?"

"Obviously you don't know what getting knocked up means on our side of the ocean."

"No. What does it mean?" Chelsea asked with knitted brow.

"It means getting pregnant," Paul laughed again.

"Good God!" Chelsea exclaimed. "You North Americans are so ruddy vulgar."

"So why am I so different?" Paul grinned.

"It's those ruddy baby blue eyes of yours," Chelsea replied. "You look so innocent in spite of the way you foisted yourself upon me last night."

"I am innocent, or was. Just a lonely soldier far from home led astray by a. . ."

"By a what?" Chelsea demanded.

Paul grinned at her and she cried, "Where's my ruddy poker, there's a burglar in my bed."

She grabbed the poker and made a mock swing at Paul. He threw a blanket over her and they wrestled around on the bed until he managed to take the poker from her and fling it aside.

"A beautiful woman who sings like an angel," Paul laughed as he tried to kiss her.

"Oh go on," Chelsea grinned as she turned her head to resist the kiss. "You meant to say that I was cheap trollop who was an easy catch."

"I meant no such thing. For a quid I could have got that down at the pub."

"You don't know how much I charge," Chelsea teased.

"What's that supposed to mean?" Paul asked as he relaxed his hold on her.

"I'll let you guess this time," Chelsea laughed as she wriggled out from under him and dashed into the main room stark naked. Paul scrambled after her and caught her in a firm hug by the sofa. "Oh Chelsea, I love you so much."

"I love you too, my darling Paul," she cooed as she relaxed in his arms. They sort of melted down onto the sofa where they made love one more time before Paul had to tear himself away to report back to base.

Chapter Ten

On the train heading back to their base, Paul's comrades for the most part were noisy and boisterous, chattering endlessly about the good time they'd had in London. Paul however, sat quietly in a moony state basking in the afterglow of Chelsea.

"Hey Rich Kid, you're not saying much about your night in town?" Curtis said.

"What's to say?"

"You didn't come back to party with the Newfies, I stopped there for a while."

"He must have found himself a woman for the night," Bob White joined in.

Paul smiled quietly.

"I think he found one all right. I'd say he's in love."

They all laughed and Paul smiled blissfully.

"I thought I saw you at that show where that girl Chelsea was singing." Dale, chimed in.

"I was there," Paul said with a dreamy smile.

"Wait a minute, you tried to go backstage and the bouncer threw you out."

Everyone laughed, and Curtis said, "I heard of that singer, Chelsea. They say she's got a beautiful voice."

"She *is* beautiful," Paul said blandly.

"Go on, you weren't with her last night?" Curtis asked.

"She's too famous to go out with a mere soldier," Dale added.

Paul smiled but said nothing.

"You know, by God, I think he was with her," Curtis said.

"He's been mighty quiet about last night," Jim

taunted.

"We were all payin' for our ladies, and he was getting his free," Dale jeered.

"Look I don't want to talk about it," Paul snapped as he turned toward the window.

"Best leave him alone, I think he's lovesick," Curtis said amid laughter.

"No use moonin' over her," Dale continued. "To her you were just a one-night stand. Chelsea can have any soldier she wants."

"I'm getting out of here," Paul growled as he rose from his seat.

"Don't take it so hard, buddy," Dale persisted "You'll probably never see each other again and you're probably one of a long line of soldiers."

This was too much. Suddenly Paul lunged at Dale snarling, "Listen Runt, I've had about enough of your lip."

"Ooh, touchy," someone said.

"Back off you guys and leave Paul alone," Curtis said as he stepped between Paul and Dale. "Hey bud, you were the one that said we shouldn't fight with each other."

Paul shrugged him off and went forward into the next coach. He discovered that it was full of the Newfoundlanders chattering away with their curious accents.

"Hey Paul b'y," a familiar voice called.

"Hey Tom," Paul smiled in turn.

"Did ye get a bit a fluff fer a goin' away present last night," Tom said cheerfully.

"Now don't you start," Paul snapped.

"Touchy, are we?" Alex said joining them.

"It's not my affair what ye did last night ye know," Tom said carefully.

"I met a girl, a beautiful girl," Paul said evenly. "I was getting a hard time about her in the other coach."

"I see. Well, I'll not bother ye den," Alex smiled. "Sit

down and we'll talk of otter tings."

When they arrived back in camp, the sergeant ordered a roll call and inspection. In a half-hour they were to be on the parade square in full combat gear. They hustled amid grumbles about having no time to rest, before getting ready for inspection. They lined up and the sergeant called out their names to make sure all had returned from leave. He slowly went down the line, inspecting their gear as other sergeants were doing with their squads. In two hours they would sail for France.

It was a hot sultry afternoon in June as the ship drew into the harbour at Boulogne. Paul's regiment was next off the ship after the Newfoundlanders. As they marched through streets of the small French city, boys in their early youth ran alongside them begging for candy, "Chocolate *monsieur*, *bonbons*." Some of the soldiers did throw candy after which the boys scrambled.

"Cigarettes *monsieur*," said a scrap of a boy who ran alongside Curtis.

"They seem awfully young to smoke," Curtis said to Paul as a youth came along side them asking for cigarettes. "He can't be more than twelve years old."

He probably won't smoke them," Paul replied. "Cigarettes are like gold, he would use them to bargain."

French girls waved and smiled at them. One girl, on a street corner they passed, drew her skirt up slightly and smiled with a wink, "*Cinq francs monsieur, oui?*"

"What is she saying?" Bob asked Paul. "Since you know some French."

"I think she can be had for five francs," Paul chuckled.

"I've seen soliciting on the streets in London, but this is ridiculous," Curtis scoffed.

"Times are tough. The French girls are getting pretty

desperate," Bob ventured "Their men are either all at the front or dead."

They marched by the railway station just as a train was pulling in. Their CO called them to temporarily halt at the station. They watched as those on board disembarked. There was a long procession of wounded soldiers from the front, some limping, some on crutches, with a leg missing, and some were being carried on stretchers. All wore solemn looks and many were clearly in pain. For better or worse, for them the war was over. The contingent of Canadians had stopped at the station both out of respect for the wounded and as part of their preconditioning for life at the front.

The Canadians then proceeded to march to the base camp at Etaples, a few miles away and only a short distance from the front. So close in fact, they could hear the pounding of cannons that rumbled like distant thunder. Here, in this vast sea of tents and stockpiles of armaments, were gathered soldiers from all over the British Empire. There were Londoners with their sharp cockney accents, turban-bearing Sikh warriors from the Punjab in northen India, disgruntled Irish conscripts who muttered among themselves that they ought to be fighting the English rather than the Germans, South Africans, Australians and New Zealanders already bloodied from the ill-starred Gallipoli campaign the previous year, the Newfoundlanders and finally, a large number of Canadians. Paul heard the skirl of bagpipes announcing the arrival of a Scottish highlander battalion These kilt-clad warriors marched through the centre of camp with great fanfare and precision as they followed their pipers.

"Look out Hun," Paul said. "The Scottish highlanders are the finest fighters in the whole empire."

"Their bagpipes alone are enough to scare the wits out of the Germans."Curtis added.

"I was reading up once, that the bagpipes are a

deliberate psychological weapon used by the British," Jim added. "People unfamiliar with the sound find the pipes very unnerving."

"I find them irritating as it is," Dale mumbled.

They would all undergo a final training at Etaples. There were marching drills and machine-gun training. This was rigorous since machine-guns were heavy weapons with water-cooled barrels and mounted on tripods. Each machine-gun was assigned a two-man team as it took two men both to carry and operate the weapon. Speed at which one could set up and man a machine-gun emplacement was critical for repelling an enemy attack. There was more training at bayonet fighting. Again they were lectured to disembowel the enemy, to never stick a bayonet in the ribs where it might get stuck.

They were issued gas masks and sent into chambers full of tear gas so they could learn the hard way, how to put them on right. One bellicose instructor lectured them in graphic detail; "Make sure your mask is always clean and that you are clean-shaven. Death by gas is the most horrible way to die. Chlorine gas will dissolve your lungs leaving you gasping for a breath. Your eyes will burn and melt right in their sockets. Indeed, your final moments on earth will be in a writhing agony that will make being burned alive seem merciful. Then there is phosgene, a gas so deadly you can't even see it and it doesn't usually kill you until several hours after you've inhaled it. If you smell bleach, it'll be chlorine, if you smell musty old hay, it'll be phosgene. Whenever the wind blows toward our trenches, you can expect gas."

If the gas lectures weren't enough, they told of more personal dangers. "Keep your feet as dry and clean as possible. Trench foot is a fungus that attacks your toes and ca uses them to rot away if not cared for. Then there are lice, to you from the outlying areas of the empire, lice is a familiar thing so I trust you will guard against it unless you enjoy scratching until your skin bleeds. Then there are rats. Rats thrive on human misery, they carry disease, and they are everywhere. They will try to eat your food and they may even try to eat you if you appear helpless in their eyes. Although they are rodents, they are omnivorous."

Upon leaving one of the more grisly lectures, Paul remarked to Curtis, "After hearing all that, being shot at by the Hun is the least of our worries."

"Yeah, it definitely takes all the fun out of going up to the front," Curtis replied dryly. "Not that there would be any fun in being constantly shot at."

"Let's go over to the vendors and see if we can get some fruit or spearmint candy," Paul said, motioning to a row of vendors that had set up near the lecture tent.

"Yeah, these Frenchmen are everywhere trying to sell you something," Curtis sighed.

"It's good they let the vendors come on base since they won't let us go into town." Paul replied.

"But they don't sell women or booze here," Curtis snorted.

"Well, we'll just have to settle for spearmint," Paul laughed. "They say it's good for trench mouth."

"Spearmint, spearmint, that's all I ever hear. They think we live on spearmint."

Presently a train whistle blew and a train went by. It was perhaps a mile long and it contained nothing but flatcars loaded with cannons of varying sizes interspersed with crates of ammo heading for the front.

"Look at all the artillery," Curtis said. "Something is up."

"I've heard rumours of a major offensive in the works," Paul said gravely. "They want to take the heat off the French at Verdun."

"I hear there are about a million French and German soldiers engaged in battle around Verdun," Curtis replied.

That night many at the camp, including Paul's regiment, were informed that they were going to the front the following morning. B and C companies of Paul's regiment were to temporarily split off from the main body of the Canadian Corps bound for Flanders, to assist the British regulars on the Somme front and would be under the command of British officers. Their first job would be to assist in ferrying ammo to the cannons. The rest of the Canadians were going to an area in Flanders to the west.

There was a general groan among those being selected and Jim grumbled, "I came here to fight a war, not be a stevedore."

"I was hoping that our regiment would stay together," Curtis added.

"Yeah," Paul replied.

"What's that soldier?" the lecturer who was also their new platoon leader, Lieutenant Bedford, said sharply, looking at Paul.

"I was hoping, sir, that we would get to fight with the rest of the Canadian Army, sir." Paul replied directly.

"As a soldier in the enlisted ranks, you will go where you are told and do what you are ordered to do," he said sharply with a puffed-up arrogance. "Is that clear, soldier?"

"Yes, sir."

"Now then, since it is your last night on base before going to the front, you will be issued passes to go into town for a few hours. They expire at midnight."

A cheer rippled through the assembly.

"Need I remind you," the Lieutenant continued ever truculently, "the penalty for being AWOL is time in the stockade at hard labour, or possibly the firing squad."

"Are you comin' to town with us tonight, Paul?" Curtis

asked later when they were all getting ready.

"I thought I'd stay back and write a couple of letters. My family and Chelsea should know that I am off to the front. I haven't had an opportunity yet to tell Ginny about Chelsea."

"But this is our last night, buddy," Curtis continued. "Maybe our last night on Earth for tomorrow we march into hell."

"I don't know about you guys, but I'm ichin' to try out some of these French women," Bob grinned lustfully.

"Or find out what their booze tastes like," Jim added.

"Are you sure you won't come?" Curtis asked.

"Nah. I must get these letters out. In case it is my last night on Earth," Paul replied.

"You always say you're gonna survive this war," Curtis continued.

"I will, but just in case."

"I think he's too lovesick to enjoy the pleasures of France," Bob laughed.

Paul smiled quietly to himself.

When he was left alone in the tent, Paul fished out his writing pad, deciding to write to Ginny first:

Dear Ginny,

Well, we arrived in France and went through some final training as tomorrow we go to the front. Fear not though, my company has been assigned to the rear area to off-load ammo for the cannons so I shouldn't be in the direct line of fire. What I really wanted to tell you though is, I think I am in love.

I have met a most beautiful girl named Chelsea who is an entertainer with an incredible voice. As she is from a so-called "lower station," perhaps it would be best if this is kept our little secret so as to not upset our parents. If this relationship unfolds as I sincerely hope it will, then I shall have to tell them. Until then, this shall be another of our untold secrets.

Paul paused before continuing, as he went on to tell Ginny about his stay with Sir Wilfred and other topics of mutual interest. After concluding that letter, he wrote a tender love note to Chelsea. With it he enclosed a copy of the photo he had taken back in Toronto. He asked for one of her in turn. With the letter complete and sealed, ready to be mailed, he lay back in his bunk in a state of bliss as he thought of Chelsea.

Later that night Paul's buddies returned in an intoxicated state as they stumbled through the words of *A Long Way to Tipperary*.

"You shoulda come to town buddy." Bob slurred. The place was crawlin' with whores everywhere."

"I trust you were satisfied," Paul grinned.

"Are you kidding?" Bob said with his thick voice. "Three brothels in town and you had to stand in line, and I ain't standing in line for no whore."

"Whores are a soldier's best friend," Paul laughed. "You guys told me that."

"Whores are a dime a dozen, or should I say a franc a dozen," Bob's words trailed off in a pathetic giggle.

"Here buddy, I brought you something," Curtis laughed as he produced a bottle of French beer from under his tunic and handed it to Paul.

"I don't know," Paul grinned as he took the bottle. "You know what happened the last time you guys offered me booze on base."

"Yeah, but the Rich Kid ain't no squealer," Jim said as he put an arm around Paul, weaving and wobbling as he did so.

Paul removed the cap from the bottle and took a large swallow, "Um, good. Better than English beer."

"Every time I think of those days, I feel foolish, " Curtis said. "We tormented you for no reason."

Paul quaffed the remainder of the bottle and set it down on the floor with a belch. "That was then and we were strangers. Now we're a team and the Hun is our enemy."

"Buddies forever," Bob declared in his drunken voice, as he extended his hand.

"Buds to the end," Curtis added.

They all slapped hands to affirm their friendship, just as the call came for lights out.

The following morning, the men of B and C company, along with the Newfoundland regiment, climbed onboard a supply train bound for Ameins near the front. They sat on open flat cars among the crates of ammunition. They were dressed in full combat gear. Their main gear consisted of a sixty-pound field pack on their backs, their utility belts with pouches loaded with rifle ammo. They also carried a trenching spade, and an issue of two hand grenades each. The field pack, among other things, carried iron rations, which were tins of bully beef and biscuits, some packages of coffee and tea, a jug of water, a medical kit and a bedroll. On their chest, they carried an ominous new piece of gear with their uniforms, a large, square cloth-like pouch containing the gas filter and behind it the respirator attached with a hose. This new peice of equipment constantly reminded them that a new and hideous kind of death awaited them at the front.

"I wish the Hun had never started using gas," Curtis said as he put a hand on his pouch. "I can understand being shot at or even having a cannon shell go off near me, but this gas. . ."

"Yeah, I'm not looking forward to finding out if I have my mask on right," Paul added.

"So what do you think of these," Bob said as he lifted the new steel helmet issued to them at Etaples. "I feel like I have a soup plate on my head."

"Yeah, they do look like soup plates alright," Jim said as he took his helmet off to look at it, and they're awfully heavy."

"You'll probably be glad to have it on with all the debris flying around," Curtis said. "They say it's better than the French helmet that looks like a fireman's hat."

"I was talking to Tom Brady last night," Bob said as he changed the subject. "The Newfies are going to the Somme also, in a sector known as Beaumont Hamel. They were also hoping to be lumped in with the Canadians. Instead they were made part of the 29th British division."

That's because they are still colonials," Paul added.

"Is that what we are," Jim scoffed. "They separated us from the rest of the Canadian Army."

"We're just loaners, I understand," Curtis replied. "Hopefully we'll join the other Canadians later."

"Yeah, we got some real jackass Limey for a lieutenant," Bob spat.

"At least we still have our own sergeant." Paul said.

"Yeah, if that one that trained us in England would a come along, I'd a shot him and said the Hun did it," Jim grumbled.

Yeah," Bob agreed. Paul looked out at the war-scarred countryside and lit a cigarette.

At the small city of Ameins on teh banks of teh actual River Somme, the boys of B and C companies were kept onboard and the flatcars with the ammo while the Newfoundlanders disembarked and marched away to their sector of the front. The flatcars were then attached to a special train that took them directly to the rear area of the front.

As they approached the front, they could hear the pounding of cannon fire with ever-increasing intensity. Also, as they neared the front, the countryside was scarred with shattered houses, broken trees and shell craters from previous engagements. When they arrived at the rear area, they could see rows of cannons as far as the eye could see, firing at the German lines without cessation. The Newfoundlanders were sent straight to the trenches, while B and C company set up camp near one of the ammo dumps, then went about their task of off-loading the trains that were bringing in the ammunition for the cannons. As there were over three thousand cannons involved in this, perhaps the greatest artillery bombardment in history, special railway tracks had been laid so that ammunition could be brought in by the trainload. Day after day, Paul and his comrades unloaded trains onto trucks and horse-drawn carts. Mostly they were explosives, but some of the shells contained poison gas and when the wind was favourable, the gas-filled shells were fired at the German trenches.

At the end of each long day Paul would literally drop into bed, but his sleep was restless with all the pounding, and the night sky was constantly lit up by hundreds of cannon muzzles spitting fire like grotesque lightning. Indeed some of the cannon barrels glowed red from so many discharges.

"There can't be anything left of the Germans by now," Curtis said one night, as they went to mess tent for supper. "How many days have we been shelling them now?"

"It must be about seven or eight now," Curtis replied. "My God, I've never seen so many cannons."

"Yeah, I've unloaded a lot of gas shells as well."

"Yeah, well if we don't blow the Hun out of their trenches, we'll gas them out," Curtis added dryly.

"Well, at least we have a lot of fireworks for Dominion Day tomorrow," Paul laughed.

"Yeah."

Chapter Eleven

The cannons were still blasting away when Paul's outfit was awakened for roll call on the morning of the First of July.

"Oh joy, another long day of unloading ammo trains," Dale complained, as they scrambled out of bed to answer the bugle.

"It's when the cannons stop, that you have to worry," Paul replied as he quickly pulled on his uniform.

"That's when we finally see action," Dale continued in an almost anxious note as he quickly buttoned up his tunic.

"You're that anxious to have your head blown off?" Curtis said dryly.

They lined up for roll call and then were dismissed for breakfast.

"Look at all the troops marching by," Paul said during breakfast in the mess tent. Its sides had been rolled up in the summer heat, so they could see what was happening outside. As long columns of troops marched by in full gear, he added, "Something is up."

"I think the long-talked-about attack is going to happen soon," Curtis replied.

"What's left to attack?" Bob scoffed. "The cannons must have obliterated the German positions by now."

"We'll probably just march forward and claim what's left of them for ourselves," Jim added.

"Maybe we'll march all the way to Belgium," Dale chimed in.

"Company C, get ready for inspection in full battle gear," their platoon leaders abruptly announced as they were finishing breakfast. "On the double."

They quickly scrambled to obey as if by automatic reaction, some leaving unfinished breakfast behind without a thought. As they geared up, the cannons fell silent.

"What happened?" Paul cried in the ear ringing silence.

"The cannons stopped firing," Curtis observed.

"The attack must be on," Bob ventured as he hitched his field pack onto his back.

"That means we'll be in it," Dale added soberly.

"You sounded excited about it before," Curtis scoffed at Dale.

"That was before. I could get killed," he observed glumly.

"That's a distinct possibility," Jim added dryly.

"A runt would probably be too small a target for their guns," Curtis added.

"Very funny," Dale snorted, as the others all laughed.

They were lined up in platoon-sized batches and as usual, the sneering Lieutenant Bedford presided over the platoon to which Paul belonged.

"Well, today you might get to be soldiers," he said with his usual disdain. "Although we expect the Hun's forward positions to be pulverized, some of the rearguard might offer resistance. However, since you are colonial dregs that are new to this game, you will be held at the rear and used to collect the dead. That is, unless the Hun offers a lot more resistance than anticipated. Then you might have the opportunity to get killed. Your assembly point will be by the forward cannons. Dismissed."

"What an ass that lieutenant is," Paul grumbled, after the lieutenant walked away.

"I'd like to see an opportunity for him to get killed,"

Dale added as they moved out to take their places.

"Yeah," Jim and Bob agreed.

Meanwhile at the front trenches at 7AM on that fateful morning, came the cry of "Over the top lads." Led by their junior officers, tommies from all over the British Empire, clad in their khaki uniforms with their *soup plate* helmets, and weighted down with a sixty-pound field pack on their backs, scrambled up the sides of their trenches and gingerly stepped over the barbed wire into no-man's-land.

"Stay in close formation with rifles out front," their officers told them. "There may be a few scattered pockets of enemy resistance. Our main mission is to secure their trenches and take prisoners of any of their troops that still might be alive."

Tom Brady of the Royal Newfoundlanders said to Alex McDonough, "Tis a pity dat de cannons done such a good job. Us Newfies came here fer a good fight."

"Yeah," Alex replied.

So a great weaving wall of tommies fifteen miles long and nearly one-hundred thousand strong, walked slowly, shoulder to shoulder, several tiers deep, with bayonet-affixed rifles out front, up a slight incline toward the German lines located on a ridge in front of them. They had been assured that no army in the world could withstand eight days and nights of continuous artillery bombardment. The capture of the forward trenches of the Hun would be a cakewalk and the heights would be theirs. Down the line from wherePaul was stationed, he could hear the skirl of bagpipes as the highlanders went over the top.

The first signs of trouble came with the realization that the enemy barbed wire was still intact. Worse, it had been lifted up by the artillery blasts then dropped again leaving it more tangled than before. As the artillery had failed to chew it up, entry into the German trenches would be difficult. Some thought they could see a stirring behind the barbed wire. Then came the awful roar of a multitude of machine-guns letting loose upon them. This, joined in chorus by gunshots of innumerable rifles, followed by trench mortars with exploding shells, and finally, their cannons let loose. Far from destroyed, the Hun had weathered the storm of the massive artillery bombardment in their concrete reinforced bunkers. When the shelling had stopped they crawled out of them to find a great wall of enemy soldiers advancing slowly toward them. They quickly scrambled to set up their machine-guns and trench mortars and were now spewing fire and lead upon the advancing army with every weapon at their disposal. The tommies began falling like ten-pins in a bowling alley. Exploding shells landing either in the midst of this advancing wall of men or in the assembly trenches behind would lift bodies, a dozen at a time, into the air and drop them helter-skelter all around.

From his place by the artillery where their outfit was held in reserve, Paul watched in horror as wave after wave of tommies scrambled over the top into no-man's-land only to be mowed down by that terrible scythe of the Grim Reaper in the guise of German weaponry.

"The Germans are cutting them down like grass," Curtis said horrifically, amidst the roar of thousands of gun discharges and exploding shells.

"That's not an attack, it's a slaughter," Bob added.

"I thought they said they destroyed the forward trenches of the Hun," Paul grumbled. "They lied to us."

"You will keep your comments to yourself soldier," Lieutenant Bedford scolded as he happened to walk by them when Paul made the remark. "By the rate that they are falling, you'll soon have your turn."

"Yes, sir," Paul replied. Though his face was frozen in the expressionless mode required, his eyes were smoldering with contempt for the irksome lieutenant.

"Now we have a good fight," Tom cried to Alex amid the din even as their fellow Newfoundlanders were dropping all around them like flies.

"Let's get the bloody Hun," Alex cried as his pace quickened and his adrenalin flowed. Tom and Alex were among the last of the Newfoundlanders to go down as they fell against the barbed wire in front of the German trenches. In the course of less than half an hour virtually all of the Newfoundland regiment had been annihilated. Only a few at the rear survived.

The call went out for C Company to move up to the front trenches. With clammy hands and knots in their stomachs, Paul and the others moved down into the rear trenches and through the connecting trenches working their way to the front line. They came to a section of trench work collapsed by German artillery. There were bodies half buried in the dirt. Sometimes a hand would be sticking out or other times a head, or perhaps a dismembered leg lying on top.

They watched with incredible horror as men, seemingly with indifferent calm, clamoured over the top only to be mowed down by enemy fire.

"Look at them still going over the top into no-man's-land to get massacred," Paul murmured. "Like lambs to the slaughter."

"Hell uva way to celebrate Dominion Day," Bob added.

"It might be our last," Dale swallowed.

"This must be how a condemned man feels taking his final walk to the gallows," Curtis replied gravely. Most of the others were too stupefied to comment further.

Responding more like robots than humans, they continued on forward. It occurred to none to do an about-face and turn their guns on the officers who ordered this insane butchery.

Paul kept telling himself silently, *'Somehow I'm going to survive this.'*

As C Company approached the final row of trenches, as if by miracle the order rang out to holdfast and for those still in no-man's-land to retreat to the trenches. The artillery resumed firing at the front German trenches to prevent them from exploiting an otherwise great opportunity that had opened before them.

Paul now saw a steady stream of wounded that were now crawling back from no-man's-land, moaning and crying, being carried by their comrades who were still able to walk. As they crawled back to safety the gunfire from the German lines slowly died down. Even in the insanity of war, there was still enough honour not to shoot wounded soldiers in the back. As Paul looked out over no-man's-land, everywhere in front of him, the ground was littered with bodies. A grizzly sea of khaki-clad bodies littered no-man's-land along the entire fifteen-mile attack front.

Stretcher-bearers and paramedics were now swarming through the trenches to try to get the wounded tended to, and moved to the back As the torrent of wounded overwhelmed the number of stretcher-bearers on hand, Paul's unit was called upon to assist.

At the rear, where an emergency field hospital was set up, overworked medical attendants were scrambling to save those who still might live. Amid the moans of the dying, all too often Paul would see an orderly draw a blanket completely over one of the casualties as death claimed another. Officers attempted to do roll calls only to find to their dismay that entire regiments had been decimated. Some regiments were annihilated by enemy cannon fire before even getting out of the trenches. The few that actually made it into the enemy trenches, such as the West Yorkshire Battalion, and the 1st Essex Regiment, were slaughtered by the defending Germans in a murderous crossfire.

In the midst of this mayhem of the returning wounded, the lonely piper who had seen most of his Scottish highlander battalion fall before him, offered a sad lament on his pipes. As he worked his way through the moving strains of *Hector the Hero,* tears welled up in the eyes of his fellow survivors as they stood rigid with right arms frozen in salute. Even non Scottish soldiers up and down the line within earshot of the pipes stood in silence. As the stirring notes reached Paul and Curtis, who were carrying an empty stretcher back to pick up more wounded, they stopped in their tracks to listen for a moment.

"Awesome," he said to Curtis. "I've never heard the pipes like this before."

"I have to admit, I never cared for bagpipes, but this touches one's heart." Curtis replied.

"It makes one want to take off his hat," Paul added.

"Shall we?" Curtis said as he removed his helmet. Paul followed suit.

"Come on you two. Get moving," the lieutenant bawled. "There's not time to dawdle; men are dying."

Paul and Curtis resumed their duties exchanging glances that reflected their shared contempt for the irksome lieutenant. They did notice however, that there were others who stopped, if only for a moment, to honour the fallen as the pipes had beckoned.

As the notes carried across no-man's-land to the German lines, soldiers who earlier exclaimed, "*Was ist der laerm?*"[1] when the skirl of bagpipes announced the

[1]*Was ist der laerm* - What is that noise?

highlanders going over the top, now stood in silence, awed by the unique way in which these proud warriors honoured their fallen. The machine gunner who, a short time before, had mowed down the kilt-clad warriors by the dozen, grew misty-eyed with the powerful strains of the pipes and slowly removed his helmet. Several of his comrades around him followed suit.

When he was off duty, Paul searched for the Newfoundlanders among the vast sea of wounded. He found the fiddler, Robbie Murphy, on a cot wrapped in bandages.

"Is that you, Paul?" he said weakly with morphine-clouded eyes.

"Yes, Robbie, it's me. Where are Tom and Alex?"

"Dead. . , they're all dead," he said sadly with laboured words. "I saw them fall. . . It was a massacre. . . They sent us all to die. . . Now I'll be joinin' them." Robbie closed his eyes and became very still.

"Robbie," Paul cried. "You're gonna live."

There was no response from Robbie and a nurse came along. Upon checking Robbie's pulse, she drew the blanket over his head. She motioned for two orderlies to remove his body so the cot could be made ready for another. All was done without a word or slightest trace of emotion. Paul wanted to complain of the seeming callousness of the situation, but as his mouth quavered and tears welled up in the corners of his eyes, he could find no words to say. Paul learned later, of the eight hundred Newfoundlanders who went into battle that day only about sixty answered roll call the following morning, their unit had sustained a greater-than-ninety-per-cent casualty rate. Indeed, of the one-hundred thousand British Empire soldiers sent over the top that terrible morning, only forty-thousand reported for duty the following day. Of the sixty-thousand casualties, twenty-thousand had been killed outright and thousands more would die in the following days.

That night, the soldiers were lectured by the company commanders about the calamitous day's events. They attempted to explain away questions as to why the Hun was not destroyed by the intense artillery bombardment, saying only that they must have extremely durable bunkers. Finally Captain Walker of C Company declared: "You must never mention a hint of today's events in letters back home. It is bad enough that the Hun can see all the bodies that litter no-man's-land, but if he should know the true scale of today's tragedy, he will think himself victorious and launch his own offensive before we can bring in reinforcements. It is also bad for morale on the home front. If anyone dares mention a hint of today's events in a negative light to those back home, it will be considered an act of treason and dealt with accordingly. You all know the penalty for treason."

"The firing squad," Dale said out of the corner of his mouth.

"That is correct, soldier," Captain Walker continued. "Since our fair company wasn't bloodied in the attack, we will do body recovery detail. It is the lot of green soldiers to be put on body recovery detail as a means of hardening you to the rigors of combat."

"Won't the Hun massacre us when we go into no-man's-land to get the bodies?" Paul ventured.

"There is an understanding from both sides that unarmed solders can go into no-man's-land to retrieve their dead. The Hun doesn't want to be overpowered by the stench of thousands of rotting corpses any more than we do. Don't worry, they'll even let us pick the ones off the barbed wire in front of their trenches if we're unarmed."

Thus, the following day, Paul and hundreds of other unarmed soldiers under a white flag, gathered up the dead under the watchful eye of the German army. Those soldiers either dismembered or otherwise badly mutilated were buried in mass graves using shell craters, once their dog tags were removed for identification purposes. The others were taken to the back for a more orderly burial. Later those bodies collected at the rear were hauled by the truckload to a special cemetery in a sandy area of Flanders where their graves would be marked by rows of simple white crosses.

For the first time Paul saw the ones they called the Hun in the distance. They wore grey-green uniforms and helmets that came down over their ears. Those not engaged in watching over the body recovery teams were busy re-excavating trenches collapsed by British artillery of the previous week's bombardment and collecting their own dead.

No amount of training, even by the most brutal of drill sergeants could prepare one for the horror of either collecting the often mutilated bodies of the dead, or of witnessing the holocaust of the previous day. None of this was envisioned in the glory of marching off to war. It would be two days before Paul could bring himself to eat again.

Chapter Twelve

When Paul's first rotation at the front trenches had ended and they had been given rest time at the rear, he composed a letter to Ginny without waiting for her reply to the last one he had written on the eve of the battle. He wanted to put the horror of combat in a lighter text. He felt he could comment on the opening events of the battle, but the later parts were either too grisly or not what the prying eyes of the army censors ought to see.

Dear Ginny,

It is now the fourth day of manning the front trenches for our outfit and I saw my first airplane. It was a German war plane, I could tell by the large black, white bordered crosses painted on its wings and fuselage. Airplanes have come a long way since they were invented back when I was a child. It is flying high over our trenches, probably spying on our positions. Then I saw one of our aircraft coming with its target ring decals.

Curtis is all excited about seeing a real dog fight. That is a term we use for aerial duels between the aviators. I consider these aviators the new knights of warfare, jousting in the skies as their medieval counterparts did on the ground. They are busy circling each other firing bursts from their mounted machine-guns. Both Curtis and I are amazed at how they were able to invent a machine-gun that can fire through a spinning propeller without hitting the blades.

I wonder if the Red Baron will show up one of these times. He is the legendary German pilot who is the terror of the skies. They say he has more kills than any other air ace. Curtis thinks that our Billy Bishop would give him a run for his money. I bet people would pay to watch a dogfight between those two. Imagine our very own Canadian pilot is the best air ace in the entire British Empire.

The aerial duel continued until the German craft was shot down. We all cheered wildly. Some even threw their helmets in the air. Then another German airplane came and shot down our victorious pilot. As his plane crashed in no-man's-land in a similar flaming plummet, we could observe wild cheering from the German trenches. Sometimes it seems that this war is some kind of grotesque game of gigantic proportions.

Soon there were several airplanes from both sides engaged in a spectacular air show and in the end our side prevailed with a superior number of kills and all the German planes retreated far behind their lines.

As soon as the dog fights died down, our artillery opened up a ferocious barrage. Curtis suspects they must have seen something to provoke an attack. The attack, my very first, is too grisly to describe and we will leave off to say that I survived in good form. As you know, dear sister, I plan to survive this war as I made you that promise. I trust all is well on the home front and that you are striving to become a debutante, ha, ha.
Love from your brother
Paul

Meanwhile, returning to the battle that followed the aerial duels, when the airplanes had cleared the area, the British artillery opened up a ferocious barrage upon the German lines. Curtis cried, "Oh, oh, they're preparing for an attack. Our boys in the air must have seen something."

"Yeah," Paul said grimly. His hands that were clutching his rifle broke out in a cold sweat.

More troops were moving up from the rear and a cry from the officers, "Fix your bayonets," was issued. Those who didn't already have their bayonets attached quickly scrambled to secure them to their rifles. An airplane flew overhead and apparently signalled as the cry that the soldiers feared worst, rang out, "All right lads, over the top!"

The reaction was automatic as the men scrambled up the pallets and through the barbed wire into no-man's-land. "Fan out," was the cry so they would be more difficult as targets. They cried out as they charged toward the German lines to stir up their adrenalin, some even chanted, "Kill the Hun! Kill the Hun!" as they ran.

They were nearly at the German lines before the artillery ceased fire, thus the Germans had little opportunity to fire back. Many of their machine-gun nests had been knocked out and this time the fire power was heavy enough to blast holes in their barbed wire. They leapt into the German trenches shooting and stabbing with a savage fury, too charged with adrenalin to know that they had been transformed from human beings into killing machines. Paul's only thought was, *'Kill the Hun.'*

They had advanced into the second row of German trenches as the Germans retreated to a more secure position. The Germans then began to return artillery fire into their former trenches. Soon the British artillery moved up to resume firing. The call went out to hold the line,thus, suggesting that they would neither retreat nor move forward. Machine-guns were quickly moved up, and not a moment too soon.

Someone cried, "They're coming! The Hun is

coming!"

Everyone scrambled to their forward positions and fired on the line of enemy soldiers charging at them. Most of the attacking soldiers either fell or dove into shell craters in no-man's-land, but none made it to the new line established by the boys of C Company. As the brief attack died down, Curtis observed, "I think the Hun doesn't have the manpower to press on."

"Keep your eyes peeled," the sergeant bawled, "There are some of them holed up in shell craters."

The din of the fighting died down as dusk began to overtake them and Paul leaned against the trench wall and lit a cigarette. The world around him was a churned up mess of dead Canadian and German soldiers all mixed together as if they had been stirred up with a gigantic bloody stick.

Paul looked at his bloodied bayonet and the blood splatters on his uniform that were not his own. "My God, I've become a killer," he muttered.

"Don't take it so hard, buddy," Curtis said, coming alongside him and casting an eye forward in case of attack. "It's either them or you, there *is* no choice, but I see you survived the attack unscathed."

"And you? You still look to be all in one piece," Paul grinned weakly. "Have you seen Bob Jim or Dale?"

"Not since we reached the German trenches."

They heard some moaning behind them and turned to see Bob helping Jim along. The right sleeve of Jim's tunic was blood soaked and his arm hung limply.

"Jim, what happened?" Paul said as they rushed to his side.

"My arm got mangled," Jim gasped. "The pain, oh the pain!"

"Just lie quietly. We'll see what we can do." Curtis

said in a comforting voice.

"Back to your posts!" Lieutenant Bedford cried harshly as he came upon the scene. "The stretcher-bearers will take care of the wounded."

All but Bob returned to their positions of watching for counterattack.

"You too!" he yelled at Bob, who was preparing a tourniquet for Jim's arm.

"He's my friend, sir," Bob pleaded. "He'll bleed to death."

"You know the rules. Wounded take care of themselves until the stretcher-bearers arrive."

"Just cinch up that tourniquet," Jim gasped, "I'll be alright."

Jim winced as Bob secured the tourniquet on his upper arm.

"Maybe you didn't hear me, soldier," the lieutenant barked. "Back to your post. Don't look at me like that, or by God you'll be on burial detail for the foreseeable future," he added, as Bob glowered at him.

"He is a friend to all of us," Paul said flatly.

The lieutenant wheeled to see who had made the comment and in return saw all faces scowling contemptuously at him in the gathering gloom. Bob slowly moved back to his position, glancing back to see if Jim was okay.

"You know the rules," Bedford continued. "I should have all of you put on report, and you," he said looking at Bob, "you especially."

He glanced again at the hostile faces of the squad members and muttered, "Canadians."

Then looking at the sky, he said, "The moon is coming out and the Hum may try to counterattack in the moonlight so keep your extra guard up. We'll be sending up more machine-guns and setting up more cannons under cover of darkness."

The Germans ceased firing their cannons, indicating that they were digging into their new positions for now. The stretcher-bearers were now moving up to collect the wounded and one pair arrived to take charge of Jim. He was given a shot of morphine to quell the pain and was taken to the rear. Since the stretcher-bearers of both sides were unarmed and identified with Red Cross arm bands, they seldom became deliberate targets of enemy fire.

So they got Jim," said a familiar voice as Dale came to join them.

"Yeah, his right arm is in pretty bad shape," Curtis replied.

"We'll all have to go visit him at the infirmary when we're off duty," Paul said. The others agreed.

"Look out! A potato masher!" someone cried, as a German hand grenade shaped roughly like a potato masher landed in the trench near them. They scrambled away from it and covered their heads with their arms as the grenade exploded. As Paul dove, he inadvertently landed half on top of the lieutenant.

As they regained their composure, Bedford complained as he brushed off his uniform, "You didn't have to cover me. I can look after myself." Paul wanted to say that it was purely unintentional, but merely frowned in silence.

Curtis cried out as he discovered two pieces of shrapnel sticking in his leg.

"Are you okay, buddy?" Paul asked. He was about to come over to his friend but the lieutenant's presence made him halt.

"I'll be all right. Get that Hun before he throws any more of them. One of them must be in one of those shell craters nearby," Curtis replied.

"Look out! Another one!" Paul cried as another potato

masher was lobbed at them. Dale quickly used his rifle butt like a baseball bat and hit the grenade knocking it high in the air where it exploded harmlessly. Bob, who saw approximately from where the grenade had come, threw one of his pineapple grenades, so named because of their appearance, in that direction. They heard an explosion and a cry of pain. He threw another one just to be sure. There was another even louder cry of pain after the explosion. They stood ready for another incoming grenade, but no more came their way, all that could be heard was the agonizing cries of a dying soldier only a few yards away.

Meanwhile, Curtis had picked the few pieces of shrapnel out of his leg and was now busy dressing the wound. "It seems only superficial," he gasped. "My puttee absorbed most of the impact."

"Good hit there, Dale," Paul remarked.

"I used to play baseball back home," Dale grinned.

"You ruddy Canadians act like this is some sort of game. Need I remind you that we are in a war, not a cricket match." Lieutenant Bedford was his usual haughty self. "Take care not to waste too many grenades. It may be a while before ordinance catches up for reissue."

"Yes sir," they all said glumly.

As they talked they could hear the pathetic moans of the German soldier who had received their grenades.

"Oh great, now we have to sit and listen to him die,"Dale added.

"If you have any sense of mercy, you would crawl over to where he is, shoot him and put him out of his misery," the lieutenant said with a grim voice.

As much as the moans of the German soldier grated on him, Paul was appalled at the lieutenant's callous statement.

"Just like putting down a wounded animal," Paul muttered.

"Listen, soldier," Lieutenant Bedford said harshly to Paul. "We're in the middle of a bloody war. It's either kill or be killed. If you were laying here in agony with a belly full of shrapnel, slowly bleeding to death, you'd beg for somebody to come along and shoot you. As it is, he did his best to try to kill you, didn't he?"

"Somebody should do something," Bob said as he heard a loud painful cry.

"You do it. Since you have such a sense of compassion, you can show it by putting that Hun out of his misery." Lieutenant Bedford, said. "Crawl over to where he is and shoot him, but keep low or their sentries will shoot you."

"M-me sir," Bob replied horrifically.

"Do it! That's an order," the lieutenant barked. "You other guys cover him. Take my pistol and leave your rifle behind, it be easier for you to do your job from a prone position."

Bob set down his rifle and grabbed Lieutenant Bedford's revolver with a fearful look in his eye while Paul and Dale scrambled into position with rifles ready. As soon as he secured his bandage with his puttee, Curtis joined them. Bob crawled out of the trench and inched forward toward the moaning soldier. In the moonlight they also noticed German soldiers previously trapped in no-man's-land crawling back to their own trenches. A burst of machine gun fire from the German side, firing over top of their returning soldiers, hit the ground around him and his comrades returned fire with their rifles over his prone body hitting some of the returning German soldiers. Bob hugged the ground desperately until the shooting had stopped, then resumed inching toward the moaning sound. They heard a single gunshot and the moaning stopped. Paul felt nauseous. A few moments later, Bob returned. He handed the lieutenant back his pistol, turned and vomited.

"Welcome to the war, soldier," Lieutenant Bedford said with a sneering laugh as he put his revolver back into its holster. He turned to Curtis and said in an indifferent tone, "Have a medic check your leg. If you get infection they'll cut if off." Then in a final moment of contempt he added, "By the way, this squad is on night watch so make yourselves comfortable. If they deem we hold this position for a while, I'll send up some barbed wire to give you lads something to do."

Lieutenant Bedford then moved out of their area to check on others of his platoon.

"A callous s.o.b., isn't he," Dale grumbled. "How could he just order you to go and shoot a wounded soldier like that."

"He laughs about it like he enjoys killing." Bob added.

"I don't like him one bit," Paul said. "He's one of those real rich kids that think they're above everyone. I've seen his kind before." He was thinking of Lieutenant Crawley.

"I know what you mean, bud," Curtis replied. "But we're stuck with him."

"Why did you protect him from the grenade?" Dale asked.

"Believe me it was purely by accident," Paul replied with gritted teeth.

"Next time I'll push him on top of the grenade and let *him* absorb the impact," Bob said bitterly.

After a long silence, Bob said with a sobbing voice, "I hate to admit it but in a way, Bedford was right. That soldier looked at me, grateful in knowing that I was going to put him out of his agony." Then with a quavering voice he continued, "Is this how we treat wounded soldiers? Put them down like an old dog?" He began crying as Curtis put a consoling arm around him.

"What the hell did we volunteer for?" Paul muttered.

"You, Rich Kid. You could have gotten a desk job," Dale said.

"Yeah, I also could have been the lieutenant ordering you to shoot the wounded soldier," Paul replied with a grim expression. "However, we are all here now, and stuck here until we either get killed or the war ends."

"What a hell of a spot we're in." Bob said as he began to regain his composure. "If we attack, the Hun will kill us, if we run away, we'll be shot by a firing squad of our own soldiers."

"All we can do is try to stay alive and look out for each other," Curtis said. "Try not to think of the German soldiers as people, but as the Hun."

"Kill the Hun, kill the Hun," Paul muttered.

About a week later after mailing his second letter home, Paul got a letter from Ginny. It was in some ways even more reassuring than the tender words of love he got from Chelsea. While Chelsea had captured his heart, Ginny shared the secrets of his soul.

Dear Paul,

Hoping all is well at the front. Mother and I are worried sick now that you are actually at the front and we try not to think of the grave danger you face every day that you are there.

Last night I went to my first official outing with Mother and Father. They feel that now I am sixteen going on seventeen, it is time to be introduced to society. There seemed to be no shortage of young men fawning over me, but most backed away when I asked if they had joined up. Most of them joked among them-

selves about having managed to avoid military service, an attitude I found disgusting in view of your brave decision. Most of them talked of frivolous things like automobiles, yachting or college antics. I couldn't imagine any that I met as ever being my beau. The girls were even worse. The ones that didn't have their noses too far in the air to speak to a mere daughter of a lawyer, could talk of nothing but fashions and vacation. None, either male or female, could talk of the beauty of a symphony or the pleasure of a good book, nor would any consider doing anything as challenging as you have, dear brother.

I am pleased that you found yourself a sweetheart in England. Father would probably be furious, and Mother disappointed that you chose a common entertainer for your lady friend, but they will never know until such time as you choose to tell them. Meanwhile, you may tell Chelsea that I look very much forward to the day when I can meet her. I have nothing but admiration for the bold independent path that you have chosen for yourself, even if it is currently a dangerous one. I, too, feel there is much more to life than parties and gaiety where everything is handed to you on a silver platter. Although I doubt that I would ever go to war, even if I could enlist, I have an inner calling that I must do something with my life that offers real challenge.

Well I have probably rambled on enough for now and will look anxiously forward to your next letter to know that all is well, and I hope very much that your affair with Chelsea blossoms into the real thing. God keep you safe at the front.

Your Loving Sister

Ginny

The Promise

After reading Ginny's letter, Paul had his first real chuckle since seeing combat. Perhaps there was a little humanity left in a world gone mad after all.

Chapter Thirteen

A few days later, Paul's outfit was given rest leave in the billets far to the rear. As these billets were tents as opposed to damp earthen dugouts, conditions seemed positively palatial. The squad members took some of this time to visit the infirmary at Ameins some ten miles behind the line. The town's cathedral had been requisitioned for this purpose with the full cooperation of the local clergy as it was a large building undamaged by the passing of hostile armies. There in the midst of a sea of cots and the perpetual moaning of men in dire pain, they found Jim.

"Hello you guys," he grinned painfully. "I see Rich Kid came too."

"How are you?" Paul said quietly. He observed that the bandages on Jim's right shoulder extended about a foot down to the end of the stump that was his right arm.

"All right except my right arm aches terribly."

"Your right arm is. . ." Bob caught himself.

"Amputated," Jim finished. "That's what they tell me, but fingers of my right hand still want to hold a cigarette."

"Do you want one now?" Bob asked.

"Yes," Jim said painfully as his arm stump moved slightly. Bob lit the cigarette and placed it in Jim's mouth.

"There it goes again, my fingers on the right want to hold the cigarette." He struggled awkwardly to manage his cigarette with his left hand. Finally he said in a mournful tone, "What am I going to do without a right arm, one my brain says is still there. I feel like I'm only half a man," he continued in his mournful tone. "What can a one armed-man do in life?"

"Hey, you're still alive," Curtis said, trying to be

cheerful. "And you'll be going home."

"Yeah, for you, the war is over," Dale added. "They'll never send you to the front again with one arm."

"Thanks for the consolation," Jim said ever morosely.

"You'll settle down in Sudbury and live to see your grandchildren," Paul laughed.

"What are you complaining about?" interjected the patient in the next bed, with a bitter voice. "The Hun blew both my bloody legs off."

They all turned and acknowledged the man who was a stranger to them. His accent revealed that he was from an English unit.

"I say you lot are Canadians," he managed a painful grin.

"Yes," Paul replied and you're from. . ?"

"I'm with the First Wessex Regiment, I am from Salisbury."

"We're from the North Ontario Regiment," Curtis replied. "We were in a skirmish with the Hun the other day. I had to pick shrapnel out of my leg and Jim here lost his arm."

"They got me, the very first day," the Englishman said. "Half our ruddy regiment was slaughtered."

"I know," Paul said gravely. "We lost all of our friends from the Newfoundland regiment."

"Bloody war, bloody Hun," the Englishman said bitterly. "Now I'll be spending my life in a wheelchair selling pencils for a living. They should have bloody well finished me off."

Paul thought of the incident with Bob and the German soldier, and the lieutenant's harsh words. For the first time since the discovery that his arm was missing, Jim realized that he could be worse off than he was.

Paul stopped a doctor who was making his rounds and asked if Jim was going to survive, and the doctor replied, "If he doesn't get infection he'll survive." Then he turned to go about his business. The doctor also informed them that their visiting time was up.

They were nearly at the door when they heard a patient call out in a laboured voice, "Private Cunningham. ., Paul, is that you?"

Paul stopped and turned. Even in its painful state the voice sounded familiar.

"Paul Cunningham. . . have a moment. . . to see your. . riding partner?"

Paul went over to the bed which contained a patient who was wrapped in bandages from head to toe, save his face. An intravenous bottle was attached to his left arm. It took Paul a moment to recognize the pain contorted face. "Lieutenant Crawley!" he exclaimed. "Sir," he snapped a salute.

"No need to salute. . . or call me sir. . .for that matter," Jonathan said with his pain-inflected voice.

"An officer is required respect," Paul replied. "You taught me that."

"What does it matter now. . . I'm dying anyway."

Paul sought words of comfort, and opened his mouth to say something when Jonathan interrupted, "You know. . .death is a great equalizer. . . it doesn't matter if you are a general. . . or private. . . the end is the same."

"But lieutenant."

"You might as well. . . call me Jonathan. It's all over anyway. . . if you should get to father's estate again. . . tell him goodbye for me. . . and may God keep him."

Again Paul was about to say something when Jonathan turned his head and was still.

An orderly came by and checked for his pulse. He quietly pulled a blanket over Jonathan's head and pulled out the intravenous needle. Two stretcher-bearers came to carry the deceased patient away.

Paul stood in silence for a long moment with hat in

hand. Then Curtis came over to him and put a hand on his shoulder. "You knew that officer?"

"Yes, he was Lieutenant Jonathan Crawley, the real rich kid I was telling you about."

As their leave was only forty-eight hours, they weren't issued passes to go into town other than to visit Jim. Between visits to Jim, they mostly just rested. When it was time to return to the trenches, their sergeant introduced them to a young soldier whose clean new uniform suggested that he was green.

"This is Willy Stark, a replacement soldier for Jim Jones." Addressing Curtis, he continued, "Private Smith, take him to your dugout. He can have Jim's bunk."

The soldier smiled at them with a cocksure confidence and Bob grumbled, "Just like that, Jim gets wounded and they give some other guy his bed."

"Easy Bob," Curtis said. "Jim will never be back to the front even if he fully recovers."

"I suppose," Bob sighed.

"The doc said he would likely survive," Paul added. "So if they sent somebody else to fight in his place, so be it." He put his hand on Bob's shoulder. While he, Bob, Curtis and Jim had all been close since his acceptance into the clique, Bob and Jim were a little closer, just as he and Curtis were. Dale was a tag along, accepted, but not particularly close to any of them.

"Okay kid, let's go," Curtis said to the young man. "This is where you learn to grow up fast."

"Hey, I'm not a kid," Willy said with his youthful voice. "I'm eighteen."

"I'm nineteen and I've aged five years over this last month," Paul added.

"I joined up to fight the Hun," Willy said confidently. "I can't wait to get to the front."

"You can't wait to die or get an arm blown off," Bob said bitterly. "You should look inside the infirmary before you go to your billet."

"Nah, I ain't goin' there, ever."

"This kid has a lot to learn," Curtis said as they walked along.

When they reached the dugout, there were several lights on as some of the squad members were still reading or writing letters. One was cleaning his rifle.

"Over there kid," Curtis said motioning toward Jim's bunk.

Willy sniffed the air which was a foul mixture of body odour, wet clothing, damp earth and the faint odour of rotting flesh. "Isn't there any ventilation in here?" he complained as he dropped his pack and rifle on the bunk.

"What did you expect, a bed of roses," the soldier who was cleaning his gun grumbled.

"Get used to it. This is home sweet home for your foreseeable future," Paul added.

"What's that horrid smell?" he complained again as he sniffed the odour of decomposing flesh. "Did something die around here?"

"Something or somebody," Dale said with a sneer. "One can't be certain."

"Don't you bury your dead?" Willy was incredulous that there could be decaying human bodies close by."

"Sometimes," Curtis replied. "Sometimes they get buried in the rubble, or blown to pieces. We don't always find all of the pieces. You'll know all about that. Green soldiers are always on body recovery and burial detail."

Willy felt a wave of nausea at the thought. To taunt him further, Dale added, "Sometimes the rats dig up the ones that are buried and eat the pieces. The other day I saw a big fat rat with someone's severed hand in its mouth, no doubt taking the hand away for supper." Willy's stomach was starting to churn.

To join in the teasing another soldier added, "When the rats find someone dead or dying they either go for the eyeballs or the tongue first."

That was too much for Willy. He sprang from his cot and dove for the door and vomited abundantly outside as the others chuckled.

After regaining his composure, Willy came back in grumbling that the mutton he had for supper had upset his stomach.

"I don't believe you guys," he retorted as he climbed back into his bunk. "You guys are just trying to scare me. Rats aren't carnivores."

"Rat will eat anything," Bob chuckled. "What's that fancy word you use for them, Paul?"

"They're omnivorous," Paul replied.

"That's it, omni. . . They're scavengers. Wait till you see one."

"Yeah, you could wake up in the night and find one staring you in the face," another soldier chuckled. "They like people, especially if you have something to eat on you."

"Aw, I ain't afraid of rats," Willy said, regaining his composure. "And I don't care about lice either. I heard all about them at base camp."

"If you get lice, you better not come near me," the soldier cleaning his rifle rumbled.

"Lights out in five," the sergeant announced. The soldiers put down their books and letters, and crawled into bed. As Willy crawled into Jim's old bunk he grumbled that it was dirty with Jim's old linen.

"Shut up kid," Bob said harshly. "You'll get a lot dirtier before you're done."

"What if he had lice?" Willy complained.

"That's it, I've had enough," Bob cried as he sprang

on top of Willy and began pounding on his face. Curtis and Paul dragged him off and Paul said, "Remember when you pounded my face? I swore I never wanted to see us fight each other again."

"But he said. . ."

Curtis picked Willy by the undershirt and said, "Jim was special to Bob and if you wanna live long enough to fight the Hun, then shut up." He dropped Willy down again and Willy crawled into bed without further complaint.

Willy proved not only to be irritating, but was not prone to sound advice. One night, Willy received a package from home loaded with cakes and chocolate-coated raisins. After he had gorged himself with them, he had to be prodded to put the remainder in a metal container to avoid attracting rats. He had been there two weeks already and had not seen any evidence of rats. Later, after it was lights out, Willy got a craving for the sweets and opened the can to help himself. Some of the cake crumbs and raisins dropped on the floor and some on his bed. In a few moments Willy fell asleep without thinking of either brushing himself off or closing his food container. The strong odour of raisins was a sure attraction for rats.

A short while later there were wild cries of, "No, no, get away from me!" issuing from Willy's mouth. Paul and others came awake with the noise and the unmistakable squealing sound of the loathsome rodents. Some lamps were lit and Paul saw several of these ugly little creatures that looked a lot like overgrown mice, scurrying for cover. There must have been a dozen of them. Soon everyone was flailing at them and trying to skewer the rats with their bayonets as they chased them out of the billet. In his panic, Willy grabbed his rifle and shot one of the rats point blank.

"What the hell you tryin' to do, you stupid son-of-a-bitch? Deafen everyone?" Curtis roared as he snatched the gun away from Willy.

"They ate all my goodies," Willy said forlornly as he noticed that his food can was now on its side and empty.

"You moron!" Curtis continued. "You left your food box open. No wonder the place was overrun with rats."

"Here Willy-nilly," Dale said as he flipped a rat he had skewered with his bayonet at Willy. Willy recoiled away from the creature as it bounced off his chest and landed on his cot.

"What the hell's goin' on?" the sergeant demanded as he entered the billet.

"This idiot left his foot locker open and was eating in bed," Curtis said. "So we had a rat attack."

"You don't listen well do you soldier!" the sergeant roared at Willy. "You were told about rats, now clean this place up on the double and give your blankets a shake outside. If you ever invite rats into your bunk again, you will be sleeping in the trenches. Is that clear?"

"Yes, sir," Willy said weakly.

Then there was the time during one of Willy's first watches at the front trenches when he stuck his head up to take a look across no-man's-land. This drew a burst of machine-gun fire from the German side. He felt something hit his helmet. Then, when safely below ground level, he removed his helmet and saw two dents, one on either side, where bullets had glanced off it.

"You're lucky you're still alive," Paul remarked.

"Keep your head down for God's sake," Curtis said. "Just peer over the top enough to see if we are under attack.

A sudden wave of anger flooded over Willy as he realized how close he had come to being killed. He grabbed his gun swung it over the top and began firing wildy at the German positions.

"You imbecile, you don't go shooting at the Hun like that!" Curtis shouted. "You'll give away our position."

No sooner had Curtis spoken, than the Germans began firing with trench mortars and the sergeant called for everyone to fall back. The artillery was called upon to return fire so the Germans wouldn't attempt to come over the top at them.

Later at a platoon lineup, they all received a lecture about giving away their position and Willy was called out by Lieutenant Bedford. "For your foolish action, soldier, you will receive ten days of Field Punishment Number One. The next time you do anything this stupid, you will be court-martialed. Is that clear soldier?"

"Yes, sir," Willy replied humbly."

Paul had heard of this brutal punishment, and the others who had actually seen it implemented felt a wave of pity for Willy.

"Follow me to the rear, to where the MP can pick you up."

Willy Stark was set up for this most brutal of disciplines offered by the British Army. He was bound to a stake in a manner resembling an ancient crucifixion and the stake was secured in the ground between two cannon emplacements in full view of the German lines. As the Germans knew those poor soldiers staked out in the open, like so many scarecrows, were on punishment, they seldom became deliberate targets. It was nonetheless extremely unnerving for the one serving the punishment to be left out in the open completely helpless as cannons fired and shells exploded all around him. For ten days during the daylight hours, Willy endured this punishment. Those that came near him could see him whimpering and sniveling and found it most unsettling.

"Only Lieutenant Bedford could be so cruel as to inflict this kind of punishment on a soldier," was the general comment from platoon members. "He would be better spending extended time on burial and body recovery detail." Willy's nights were spent in the stockade where he had to be dragged out the following morning begging for mercy as he was bound to his stake. He was finally returned to his comrades, a whimpering cringing wreck.

If Willy Stark learned anything from his ordeal, the lesson did not last. One morning after wake-up call with the soldiers of the squad undertaking their morning shave, Willy declined the ritual. Paul, who was shaving, said to Willy, "I'd shave too, if I were you. You never know when you'll get gassed."

Willy ran his hand over the patchy stubble of his youth on his face and shrugged. "I had more whiskers when they put me through the test chambers and I never smelled a thing. My mask fits real good." Then with a laugh he added, "I'm surprised you guys haven't told me I'm too young to shave yet."

"The thought had crossed my mind," Bob said in a low voice.

"But this is a matter of life and death," Paul added.

"Ah, I ain't gonna die today," Willy said confidently.

After roll call and breakfast, they went to take their positions at the front trenches as first watch. They were there for about an hour when Willy said, "What's that smell? It smells like old rotten grass."

Curtis looked over the edge of the trench and cried, "Oh my God, gas!"

A faint almost invisible mist was rolling toward them. All scrambled to quickly put on their respirators as a deadly cloud of phosgene gas was creeping along the ground.

Most of them scrambled quickly up onto the rear parapet to avoid the worst of the heavier-than-air gas. This in turn drew a strong burst of machine gun fire from the enemy line inflicting several casualties. Willy stayed in the trench to avoid being shot at, but was fully enveloped in gas. He appeared unaffected as the gas cloud slowly dissipated. He was however, among the first to remove his respirator as he felt a desperate urge to cough.

"God that smell stays with you," he gasped between coughs.

As the day wore on, Willy's coughing fits grew more acute and at one time he gasped and admitted, "I think I must have caught a little gas."

"You should go to the medical station and have it checked out," Paul advised.

"Nah, I'll be all right," Willy coughed. "If they see my stubble they'll reprimand me."

By late afternoon Willy was coughing steadily as he lay doubled over on the duckboards. Blood was trickling out of his mouth as the gas was slowly destroying his lungs.

"Call for the stretcher-bearers," Curtis said to one of the other squad members.

"No, no," Willy choked amid a coughing fit so severe that he was pounding on the boards. Dale bolted to do the task.

When the stretcher-bearers arrived, Willy was thrashing about in wild convulsions. In a moment he lay still with mouth wide open. This phosgene gas, the most insidious of the toxins that the combatants hurled at each other, had done its work.

"Not even Willy Stark deserved to die that way," Bob grimaced as the stretcher-bearers picked up Willy's body.

"Poor Willy Stark," Paul added quietly. "He just wouldn't listen."

Chapter Fourteen

As a reward for service and experience, Paul, Bob and Dale were promoted from private to lance corporal and were issued a set of single stripes to be sewn on the sleeves of their tunics. Curtis, because he was deemed to have leadership qualities, was accorded rank of full corporal and thus got two stripes for his tunic arms. Although Bedford had grumbled that none of them were worthy of promotion, losses in their ranks dictated that experienced men be promoted and Bedford grudgingly conceded that Curtis deserved special attention.

On the battle front, the next few weeks after the gas incident, the sector of the front where Paul's squad was stationed was relatively quiet save for a few skirmishes involving night reconnaissance patrols from both sides. Other areas along the Somme front however, had the usual see-saw battles with their attendant high casualty rates.

Then one day the Germans opened a ferocious artillery barrage in Paul's sector. The German artillery was relentless as they hugged the forward edge of their trench wall. Shells often dropped right in the trenches, hurtling bodies upward with each impact, or would strike near the trench wall causing it to collapse, leaving soldiers half buried in the dirt. The whole experience was very unnerving as one never knew where the next shell would strike.

Then someone cried, "They're coming. The Hun is coming!" Machine gunners scrambled to their positions and Paul, like the others, peered over the trench and through the barbed wire. A great wall of soldiers with their olive-coloured trench coats and coal scuttle-shaped helmets were coming toward them, shooting as they held their rifles out front and yelling with adrenalin-charged lungs as they ran toward the Canadian lines. Paul fired again and again watching them fall, but there were too many. Soon they were leaping over the barbed wire and into the trenches. Again the world went mad as men, strangers to one another, began bayoneting each other with murderous ferocity. One German soldier sprang over top of Curtis and he stabbed upward with his bayonet feeling it pierce the flesh as the soldier fell on top of him. Paul shot one who was trying to leap over him as the first wave of the German attack was now moving behind them. Paul was struck with the awful thought, *'I'm now behind enemy lines. Will they kill me or take me prisoner?'*

For a long time he lay with the dead weight of the fallen soldier on top of him and then he heard a moan beside him.

"Curtis?" he cried as he rolled the soldier off the top of him, thinking his buddy may be hurt.

He heard the moan again and realized it was from the soldier that lay over Curtis with Curtis's bayonet sticking up through his shoulder. He grabbed the soldier and pulled him away from Curtis causing the soldier to cry out in pain as this action allowed Curtis's bayonet to be withdrawn from his shoulder.

"Why didn't you shoot that damned Hun?" Curtis gasped as he struggled to regain his feet noticing the enemy soldier beside him was grimacing painfully.

The solider groaned again as he looked at them with appealing eyes. He was bleeding profusely from the shoulder wound.

"I think we are now behind their lines," Paul replied.

"Not for long," Curtis said as they heard the return of the battle. German soldiers were now retreating, leaping over the trenches to get back to their own line. The tommies, however, didn't follow. The Germans then turned and fought leaving Paul, Curtis and the wounded soldier in no-man's-land caught in a crossfire that raged over their heads. Paul turned now to the wounded solider as blood was showing through his trench coat. With his helmet long since fallen off, the soldier looked so much like themselves - a young man who had probably, like them, volunteered to serve his country. Paul remembered the time that Bob was ordered to execute a wounded German soldier. He was now determined to save this one.

"Let me help you," Paul said with kindly eyes as he moved to unbutton the soldier's coat, while Curtis watched warily with rifle in hand as he kicked the soldier's rifle out of reach.

Offering no resistance, the man said with a look of gratitude, "*Danke.*"

"Do you understand me? I want to tend to your wound," Paul said as he opened the coat.

"*Ja*," he replied. Then with broken English he continued with a painful voice. "I vas studying English in ze university before I choined up."

"That will make things easier," Paul smiled. "You are bleeding quite badly. Let me cut open your tunic so I can put a compress on the wound."

"*Danke*, I mean zhank you," the soldier said as he allowed Paul to cut open his tunic with his pocket knife so he could dress the wound.

Curtis set his rifle down and lit a cigarette, convinced that the wounded German soldier was harmless. Observing that the soldier was watching him with hungry eyes, Curtis pulled out his cigarette case and said, "Would you like one?"

"*Bitte,* I mean please," the soldier said with a painful smile.

Curtis lit the cigarette and passed it to the soldier who then began puffing gratefully.

"That's it, just lean back and relax," Paul said in a soothing voice as he put a compress on the wound. "I think the bleeding has slowed down."

"You are very kind, Englishman," the soldier said.

"We're not English. We are Canadians."

"Ah Canadians. I haff two cousins in Canada. I wonder if zhey are in your army shooting at us?" He laughed and winced with pain.

"Who knows?" Paul smiled. "Where in Germany are you from?"

"Hamburg, a big port city in norzhern Chermany. Und you?"

"Toronto, a city in central Canada."

"I'm from Winnipeg in western Canada," Curtis added.

"I zhink my cousins vent to British Columbia."

"That's in the far west of Canada."

"What is your name?" Paul asked. "I am Paul Cunningham."

"Kurt Schmidt."

"Kurt Schmidt!" Curtis exclaimed. "My name is Curtis Smith. It is almost the same name."

"It is ze same name," Kurt replied. "Did you know zhat Chermans und Englishmen are cousins anyvay?"

"Yes, our kings are for sure," Paul laughed.

"Yes, your Kaiser, our King George, and the Russian Tsar are all grandchildren of Queen Victoria," Curtis added.

"I wonder vhat ze Old Lady would zhink to see that zis family feud among her grandchildren is costing millions of lives," Kurt said as he winced from the pain.

"Sad isn't it?" Paul frowned. "Here we were strangers without quarrel, trying to kill each other. Now we are tending your wounds."

"Take off ze uniforms und ve are all people vis ze right to live in harmony," Kurt observed. "Men above us, chenerals," he snorted, "order us to kill each ozher."

"I wanted to kill you when Paul dragged you off me," Curtis added. "Now I couldn't kill you, even if ordered to do so."

After a time of listening to the battle raging around them, Curtis asked, "Did you volunteer or..?"

"*Ja*. I volunteered to serve ze *Vaterland* und His Majesty, Kaiser Wilhelm II. Und you?"

"I volunteered to serve the Dominion of Canada and his cousin, King George V of the British Empire,"Curtis replied. "I'm sure we both pray to God for victory."

"*Ja*, ve ask *Gott* for ze strength to kill each ozher," Kurt spat.

After a few moments of silence, listening to the battle raging around them Paul said, "I saw on postage stamps of the collection I once had as a child, that Germany is called *Deutsches Reich*. What does that mean in English?"

"Ze closest it means in English," Kurt replied, "is Cherman Empire."

"Then Austria which is called Oesterreich, means. . .?

"Eastern Empire," Kurt replied. "Austrians und Chermans are ze same people. Zey are of ze old empire, ze First Reich. Our new Chermany is ze Second Reich."

"Interesting," Paul replied. "And the title Kaiser is. . ?"

"Emperor or more precisely Caesar," Kurt replied with a wince as he shifted position. "Just like his ozher cousin, ze Russian Tsar means Caesar in zhere language."

"Quite a history lesson we're getting here," Curtis remarked.

"Yeah, I always enjoyed history," Paul added. "Perhaps if more people studied it, there'd be less wars."

They listened in silence for a while as the battle raged around them. Then the tommies began arriving, leaping into the trenches around them to secure the line. Curtis joined the line to repel any counterattack, while Paul still tended to Kurt.

"What's that Hun soldier doing here?" one of the others cried upon seeing Kurt.

"He is my prisoner," Paul said calmly. "I'm tending his wounds."

"What's going on here?" Lieutenant Bedford said, upon

arriving at the scene.

"This soldier is my prisoner, sir," Paul said directly as he stood up. "He was wounded so I dressed the wound."

"You should have shot him. Prisoners eat our rations," the lieutenant said with cold indifference.

"I couldn't do that, sir, with his helmet off and gun taken away, he is a human just like us."

"Human, just like us, huh. What if I were to order you to kill him?"

"Please don't put me in that position, sir," Paul begged.

Kurt looked around with fearful eyes. Was this megalomaniac going to execute him?

The other soldiers in the vicinity were platoon members who looked scornfully upon the belligerent British lieutenant at the best of times. They were appalled at the turn of the conversation. Many of them turned from their watch in disbelief.

"Get back to watching for this Hun's buddies," Lieutenant Bedford barked. "This is not your affair."

All turned forward toward no-man's-land except Curtis, Bob and Dale who watched events unfold from the corner of their eyes.

"Now then, soldier," he said to Paul. "It has been observed for some time that you have been soft on the Hun."

"Soft on the Hun, sir? I do my part when we are in battle, sir," Paul replied.

"Why are you then busy trying to save this Hun when you could have finished him off?"

"I saw a wounded soldier get executed once, and I didn't want to see it again, sir."

"If you recall, I ordered him shot as an act of mercy," the lieutenant replied.

"Kurt is not mortally wounded, sir."

"Kurt is it? He is still the enemy." Lieutenant Bedford turned to Kurt and said harshly, "How many tommies have you killed to date, Hun?"

"How many Germans have you or I killed, sir?" Paul asked blandly.

"Enough!" the lieutenant bawled. "I should order you to shoot this soldier just to remind you whose side you should be on."

Paul stood in silent disbelief while Kurt's eyes darted from one to the other.

"That's it. I order you to execute this Hun."

"I won't do it, sir."

"You refuse?" the lieutenant said in disbelief. "You refuse a direct order from an officer. Do you really know the penalty for that?"

"I am not a murderer, sir."

"Murderer, indeed. These animals have killed millions of tommies including my best friend. He died in agony from a gas attack. You want to show them mercy. Hah! The only good German is a dead German." Lieutenant Bedford had a trace of emotion in his voice with the last statement. "You Canadians think you can make up your own rules." Lieutenant Bedford was now worked up into a frenzy fuelled by his emotions. " I am your commanding officer, I order you to shoot that Hun." He looked at the anxiously watching Kurt with hatred-filled eyes.

"I will not do it." Paul was adamant.

"You are disobeying a direct order?"

"Yes, sir."

By now several of Paul's comrades were watching the tirade in disbelief. Disbelieving both the lieutenant whose sanity was now in open question and Paul's daring defiance.

"You all saw this, this insubordination," the lieutenant bawled with the tone of a madman.

All except Curtis and Bob turned back toward watching no-man's-land. Lieutenant Bedford looked around desperately, knowing that at any hypothetical court-martial they would testify against rather than for him. Yet, his obsessive hatred for German soldiers and current emotional state clouded all reason.

"All right, then I will do it." Lieutenant Bedford drew his revolver.

Paul stepped in the way and said, "You'll have to shoot me first, sir."

"If that's what it takes," the lieutenant's eyes were wild like a madman as he raised his pistol.

Paul lunged at him and tried to wrestle the pistol away. It fired, but the aim was up in the air. As they struggled, rolling around in the mud, the lieutenant gasped, "I'll have you shot for assaulting an officer."

"To make it stick, you'll need witnesses," Paul gasped as he tried mightily to wrestle the pistol from the lieutenant.

The pistol fired again and suddenly the lieutenant was still. Blood trickled from his mouth. There was a bullet hole in the side of his head.

"Oh, my God!" Paul gasped as he rose to his feet. "I've killed an officer. I'll be condemned to the firing squad."

"It was an accident," Curtis said in a comforting voice. "He had quite clearly lost his mind."

The others were all watching again and Curtis said loudly to them, "The Hun shot him when he stuck his head up."

"Yeah, the Hun shot him," Bob added. "I saw him stick his head up."

The others all agreed. The loss of the difficult lieutenant would scarcely be mourned and certainly none would want to see Paul put up against the wall for his part in it.

"You'd better take your prisoner back to the holding area," Curtis said quietly to Paul. "Take your rifle along and make like you're guarding him. I'll inform the sergeant of the lieutenant's death by enemy fire."

"Thanks, buddy," Paul replied.

Paul helped Kurt up. The latter was wide-eyed with disbelief at what he had witnessed.

"Let's go," Paul said, picking up his rifle.

"May I put *mein* hat on," Kurt said as he struggled to retrieve his cloth cap from under his coat.

"Go ahead," Paul said. Kurt got his cap out, wincing painfully as he did so, then placed it on his head. "Now I can surrender like a proper soldier."

"I should zhank you very much," Kurt said, as they walked along. "You are a very brave, but foolish soldier. *Mein Gott*, if zhey find out, zhey vill shoot you. I know zhey vould in ze Cherman Army."

"They would here too, if they determined that I murdered the lieutenant," Paul said gravely.

"Ze ozhers vill stand mitt you, *ja?*"

"I think so. It was an accident anyway, as I didn't really intend to kill the lieutenant.

"*Ja*, it vas accident."

As they reached the prisoner collection area behind the last row of cannons, Paul saw another dozen or so German prisoners, some like Kurt were wounded.

"Well, in a way you are luckier than me," Paul said. "For you the war is over."

"*Ja,*" Kurt replied. "But I vill be in a prison far from *mein* family."

"When the shooting stops, they will probably allow you to return home."

"Vell, I vish you luck und hope you survive zis var," Kurt smiled weakly. "Und ze ozher problem."

"I plan to," Paul assured him. "I promised my sister that I would return."

"We'll take over now," said one of the guards assigned to handle the prisoners.

As Paul stepped back, Kurt turned and said, "*Auf weidersechen, mein freund.*"

154

The company CO, Captain Walker, had been out and about when Paul brought Kurt to the rear. He watched silently, observing the apparent camaraderie between the soldier and his prisoner. He noticed that Paul's uniform and even his face was plastered with mud, while Kurt's uniform was only moderately dirty.

He was still out and about when the stretcher-bearers came by with Bedford's body. He was also coated with mud from head to toe, save for the little red hole in the side of his head. His right hand placed on top of his mid section was still clutching his service revolver.

"What happened to the Lieutenant?" he asked the bearers.

"He was killed, apparently by a sniper, sir," one of them said. "The sergeant will probably have a report."

"Yes, I'm sure he will." the captain replied.

"What are we to do with his body, sir? Send it on to Flanders for burial?"

"Just clean it up and bag it for now. He's from a rich family; they'll probably want to bury him back in England in the family plot."

"Yes, sir."

Captain Walker puffed on his pipe for a long moment. It was curious that a mud-covered soldier brings in a prisoner, talking to him as if he were his best friend. Then a mud-covered lieutenant comes in on a stretcher with a bullet hole in his head and clutching his pistol in his hand. Very interesting indeed.

Chapter Fifteen

That evening when they were about to leave mess tent following supper, the sergeant called Paul aside. "The company commander would like a word with you, Cunningham."

"Captain Walker?" Paul said apprehensively

"Yes, he is still our commander," the sergeant replied sardonically.

"What did you do, Rich Kid?" Curtis asked with a laugh, although his eyes were still with concern.

"Nothing," Paul replied with a trembling voice, wondering if someone had squealed.

"Don't worry, buddy," Curtis assured him. "He didn't send the MP to arrest you."

"True, he didn't," Paul said in a small voice.

Paul made his way to the tent complex that was the company command headquarters. When a guard stopped him, he explained that the captain had sent for him. After confirmation with the captain, the guard showed him the way. He stepped carefully into the captain's tent and saluted, "Lance Corporal Cunningham reporting, sir."

"Come in, solider, and be seated," the captain said after returning the salute, though he remained seated. Paul looked carefully around to see if there were any military police standing by, ready to lead him away in cuffs. "I say, you look a lot cleaner than this afternoon when you brought that prisoner in."

Paul grinned uncomfortably and replied, "It was quite muddy in the trenches where we were, sir. When the Hun came in at us, the one I bayonetted fell on top of me, knocking me into the mud."

"Indeed."

Captain Walker packed his pipe and lit it, puffed for a few moments then said, "you are Lance Corporal, Paul Cunningham." He glanced down at an open file on his desk.

"Yes, sir."

"From Toronto."

"Yes, sir."

"How did you come to be in a North Ontario regiment?"

"I don't know, sir. I volunteered for the army and this is where they placed me."

"I see. So, you've seen action since the first of July."

"Yes, sir."

It seems you are a very compassionate man. Almost too compassionate to be a good soldier.

"I try to do my duty as a good soldier, sir," Paul said ncomfortably.

"Yes, we can find no fault with your record." Captain Walker puffed on his pipe for a few moments and then continued. "Do you have feelings for the Hun? Do you see him as a human being or the enemy?"

"It depends, sir." Paul replied

"Depends? Explain soldier."

"When they are shelling or shooting at us they are the enemy. When they are trying to kill me or my friends, or anyone in the Canadian Army, they are the enemy, and I will do my best to try to kill them."

"But when one of them is lying wounded, they are peoplc," the captain interjected.

"You are referring to my prisoner this afternoon, are you not, sir?"

"Yes, the one who called you *mein freund*."

"I suppose he called me friend because I dressed his wound, sir." Paul said evenly. "After all we are a civilized country that believes in taking prisoners."

"Yes, we are," Captain Walker replied. "Even the Hun

takes prisoners."

"But you must also remember the larger scope of things. It was they who overran the small innocent nation of Belgium. It was they who sank the Lusitania and it was they who introduced poison gas to warfare."

"I am aware of all of that, sir," Paul replied. "And this is why they, as a whole, must be stopped."

"Lieutenant Bedford, I understand, was killed by enemy fire this afternoon, was he not?" the Captain asked carefully.

Paul swallowed and replied, "Yes sir, he was." Since the lieutenant was his personal enemy, he wasn't lying totally.

"Did you see him get killed?"

"Not directly, sir," Paul replied evenly. Again Paul was able to escape with a half-truth. "Lieutenant Bedford was not popular with the men under him, was he?"the Captain continued.

"I don't know, sir. He was an officer and I had to obey him, sir."

"I see," Captain Walker puffed on his pipe for a moment, then resumed. "I have been a professional soldier all of my adult life and have studied military history extensively. In every war, unpopular and incompetent officers have an extremely low survival rate. Often they die from a gunshot wound in the back."

Paul remained silent.

"That is one reason why the drill sergeant who gives basic training never goes into battle with the men that he trained." the captain continued. "Lieutenant Bedford, God rest his soul, was not a professional soldier, but one with a bought commission due to family connections."

Paul thought of his father offering to use family connections to make him an officer.

"I have observed for some time that the lieutenant had a cruel and callous streak. I should have transferred him before.

.. he got killed by enemy fire."

Captain Walker puffed on his pipe for a few moments. He studied Paul intensely then continued. "Our company has been through a lot since that disastrous first day, so I requested a ten-day furlough for the entire company, which regimental headquarters has approved. You won't have time to go back to Toronto, but you can go to either England or Paris."

Paul let out a great sigh and smiled as he said, "England will do nicely, sir."

The captain chuckled. "I presume you have a sweetheart in England."

"Yes sir," Paul smiled wryly.

"While you are there, take time to pause and reflect," the captain said in his grave tone. "Think about this war and why you joined up."

"Yes, sir.

"Dismissed."

Paul saluted, turned and left the tent.

When Paul returned to his billet he was assailed by comments like, "Did you escape from the stockade? I see you weren't arrested. What did the Captain say?"

Paul shrugged and said, "The Captain just wanted a chat. He thinks I'm too compassionate with the enemy."

"So you are," Bob said with a laugh.

Paul turned to Curtis and said quietly, "I think he suspects what happened. He's been around a long time."

"He also can't prove anything."

"What if somebody snitches?" Paul worried.

"Who would? Besides if worst comes to worst, we will all testify that in the struggle to wrestle a gun from a madman, Bedford was accidently shot. That is the truth, you must not feel guilty about an accident."

"Yeah," Paul sighed as he sat down wearily. "Even at that, I could be sentenced to hard labour for striking an officer."

"Maybe not if it was determined that he was crazy, and he was," Curtis assured him. "Anyway, since you are here and not in the stockade, they aren't going to make an issue out of it."

"Yeah," Paul sighed.

"So. I presume that you heard that we all got a ten-day furlough?" Curtis said with a grin.

"Yes, the whole company got the time off, including me, believe it or not."

"So, there you go," Curtis said. "I suppose you're going to go to England to see Chelsea?"

"You bet," Paul smiled for the first time since arriving at the billet. "And you?"

"Most of us are going to see gay Paree. "It's only a couple of hours by train from here."

"Paris sounds exciting. I've never been there," Paul replied.

"You mean you're a rich kid and you've never been to Paris?"

"This rich kid hardly got out of Canada. We only went to England once and to Boston a couple of times."

"Amazing."

"I'm going to England also," Bob said. "Jim is still there recovering and I would like to see him. I'll go to Paris next time."

"Yeah, I thought I'd drop in on Jim also," Paul added.

Although his reprieve was a short ten days, Paul felt an enormous breath of fresh air upon reaching English soil at Portsmouth. He did not breathe easy until they had safely landed in England. While Lieutenant Bedford's death was an accident, still there was the lingering possibility that word of their struggle would get out and he'd be arrested and tried at a court-martial.

Paul and Bob checked in on Jim together at the army

hospital where he was recovering. They found him in a lounge area, seated in front of a blackboard practicing writing lessons. The right sleeve of his tunic hung loosely. Upon seeing his buddies he set down his chalk and they exchanged loud greetings. He rose from his chair and gave a one-armed hug to each of them.

"Say you're looking better now," Paul laughed.

"Did they put you back in school?" Bob asked with a grin as he observed the blackboard filled with clumsily written words..

"Yeah, sort of, they're making me learn to write with my left hand," Jim replied. He picked up the chalk and wrote each of their names.

Not bad," Paul laughed. "I can almost read it."

"Never mind, they're even teaching me how to paint. Say, have either of you got a smoke?"

"Yeah, I got plenty," Bob said drawing one out of his cigarette case.

"Let's go outside. You can't smoke in here."

"So, do they let you out at night?" Bob asked as they went out to the courtyard.

"Oh yes, but only for a few hours, although I'm coming along quite well," Jim replied. "They're sending me home to Canada next week."

"Wonderful!" Bob said. "I wish I was going with you."

"Somebody has to stay and fight the war," Jim laughed. "I can't use a rifle with one arm you know."

"Yeah, yeah," Bob replied. "Say, would you like to go downtown with me tonight. I'll treat you to one of the ladies."

"Do you think they'll like a one-armed man?"

"They'll like anybody with money and cigarettes."

"What about Paul, or is he still after that singer dame?" Jim grinned at him. "What was her name again?"

"Chelsea. I'll be going to find her right after I leave here."

"Still the lovesick rich kid," Jim laughed.

"Yeah, I guess," Paul sighed.

Later Paul arrived at the theatre where Chelsea's company was entertaining. He took a seat near to the front. A tenor was singing, *Roses Are Blooming in Picardy*.

'*Fat chance of that,*' Paul thought. '*Nothing will bloom in Picardy. It probably has the same churned-up moonscape as the sector of the front where I am stationed.*'

The next number featured the troupe including Chelsea and they sang the lively lighthearted *K-K-K- Katy* as they marched around the stage. Paul's heart was pounding as he watched her. The troupe performed a few numbers without Chelsea, then finally Chelsea came on solo amid wild cheering and whistling from the crowd. Paul felt a twinge of jealousy run through him at all the attention that Chelsea was getting from the males in the audience.

Instead of a ballad, Chelsea sang a lively wartime tune, *Pack up Your Troubles in Your Old Kit Bag*.

It was amazing how they could reduce all the trials and tribulations of a soldier at the front by singing, '*Pack up your troubles in your old kit bag and smile, smile, smile,*' Paul thought. '*If only it were that easy.*'

At the end of the song Paul stood up cheering and clapping as he moved toward the stage. Chelsea noticed him, the word Paul was on her lips and she broke into a broad smile as she made her bow. She motioned for him to meet her backstage as she exited the stage. As he tried to get backstage, again the bouncer stepped in his way.

"I say, didn't I throw you out once before, a while back?"

"But Chelsea wants to see me."

"That's what they all say."

162

"Please let the soldier in," Chelsea demanded as she came up behind the bouncer.

He turned aside and Paul stepped past him into Chelsea's waiting arms.

"Oh Paul darling, I wondered if I'd ever see you again," Chelsea said, pressing her cheek on his after a lengthy kiss.

"Oh Chelsea, I've missed you so much." Paul kissed her again.

"Bloody hell, what's going on here," said a firm voice behind them. They turned and Chelsea introduced Paul to her manager, Chas Williams.

He barely acknowledged Paul and continued, "I say, this is the entertainer's area, not a lovers' lane."

"Paul's just back from the front. I haven't seen him since June," Chelsea replied. Her arm was still around Paul's waist.

"I can go back and wait for the show to be over," Paul offered.

"I don't have any more numbers tonight," Chelsea said. "May I leave with Paul now, since you gave me a whole week off anyway?"

"You've got a week off?" Paul was elated. "I have a ten day furlough."

"How grand. We can go to Dover and meet my parents. I haven't been home since Spring."

"Could you wait outside, soldier?" Chas said, somewhat more pleasantly.

"Certainly," Paul said as he headed for the backdoor.

When Paul was outside, Chas drew Chelsea aside and asked her frankly, "How serious is this affair with the soldier?"

"Quite serious, I should think," Chelsea replied. "How does this concern you?"

"You have a great future ahead of you as an entertainer. Soon we will move out of this hall and go on the road.

We may go to the front to entertain the troops or to Paris. When this confounded war is over, we may even go to New York."

"All of this sounds grand," Chelsea replied, "but what about love? I'm in love with Paul."

"In love with Paul? He's still wet behind the ears," Chas continued. "How old is he?"

"Nineteen. Why are you asking so many personal questions?"

"You are twenty-two and you want to throw your life away for a ruddy young pup of a soldier who will probably leave you a widow before this war is over?"

"Widow? I don't recall him asking me to marry him."

"Inevitably he will though."

"And if he does, it will be my affair. So, if you will excuse me, I will take my well-deserved leave now."

"Mind what I've told you, and give it some thought," Chas called after her as Chelsea went into her cubicle to get her belongings. "Please give it some thought. You have a good career ahead of you," he continued when she re-emerged from her cubicle.

"I promise I'll give it some thought. I will see you in a week's time." Chelsea stepped out the backdoor.

Paul was there waiting. He dropped the cigarette he had been smoking and Chelsea tucked her arm around his.

"I take it that your boss thinks you could do better than have a soldier for your boyfriend," Paul chuckled.

"My boss is afraid I'll run off with you and he'll have to find another singer."

"I can understand his concern," Paul replied as they walked along.

"Oh now don't you start in on me," Chelsea scolded. "Or I'll ruddy well go back in there and sing my life away."

"We wouldn't want that. Say, it's quite a coincidence

that you have a week off when I have some leave."

"Yes, its simply marvelous. You didn't mention any leave in your letters. I nearly choked up when I saw you standing there cheering me on."

"I was insanely jealous of all your other fans. The crowd loves you. As for the leave it was a surprise to me. A sort of last minute thing by our company commander."

"That was considerate of him."

"Yes, well it might be the prelude to another offensive. There are a lot of rumours floating around."

"Oh Paul," she clutched his arm more tightly. "There'll be shooting and you might get killed."

"There has already been plenty of shooting, and I'm still alive," Paul laughed. "Are we going to hail a cab, or are we going to walk all the way to your flat?"

"It's a nice night to be walking," Chelsea said with a teasing laugh.

"You're off your rocker. I've done so much walking, or should I say marching, already."

A cab came by and Paul hailed it.

"So when are we leaving for Dover?" Paul asked when they were seated in the cab.

"We can catch the train tomorrow morning. It will take two to three hours to get there."

"From Victoria Station?" Paul asked.

"Yes. Why do you ask?"

"I have my duffel bag stashed in a lock-up there."

"My, our situation is just full of coincidences today," Chelsea laughed.

"Must be our lucky day," Paul smiled.

Soon the cab arrived at Chelsea's apartment building. Paul jumped out first, helped Chelsea out and paid the fare.

"I suppose you plan to spend the night," Chelsea said with a crooked grin as the cab pulled away.

"Unless you'd rather I spent the night downtown with

one of the painted ladies," Paul teased.

"Oh, get out," she scoffed. Paul caught her by the arm and they enjoyed a lengthy kiss on the sidewalk in front of her apartment.

*   *   *

Meanwhile Captain Walker was called to the office of the regimental commander, Colonel Wilson. "This Lieutenant Bedford's father not only wants his body returned to England, but wants an inquest." Wilson stated

"An inquest sir? Imagine if the family of every soldier killed wanted an inquest."

"Not every soldier has as rich and influential a family as does Bedford. Fortunately."

"Can't he accept the fact that his son was a casualty of war?"

"Apparently not. Grief can do strange things. Perhaps it is as well?"

"Sir?"

"When they cleaned up his body for shipment back to England, the army undertakers expressed surprise that there was such a small bullet hole in his head and no exit wound on the other side. A bullet from a mauser[1] usually makes a big hole and goes right through."

"Are you suggesting. . ?"

Captain Walker began to recall the mud-coated body of Lieutenant Bedford being brought in on the stretcher, his hand still clutching his pistol.

"He was still clutching his pistol when they brought him in, sir."

"After the matter of the small bullet hole was brought up, we checked his pistol. There were two shots fired from it."

[1]Muaser - a German army rifle

"It seems unlikely, sir, that he would engage the enemy with a pistol."

"Precisely."

Captain Walker also thought of the mud-caked lance corporal who had brought in the prisoner earlier. His gut feeling had caused him to interview Cunningham, but the lance corporal betrayed no guilt. He let matters be because of Bedford's unpopularity, and the statistical low survivability of unpopular officers. Besides, Bedford wasn't shot in the back.

"Are you suggesting foul play, sir?"

"Let's say, I'll be calling on the provost marshal to look into the situation."

"I suppose, " Captain Walker sighed. "Here, I was ready to write him off as a mere casualty of war."

"Normally I would have left it at that, but for his father demanding an inquest. And if there was foul play, then those responsible will have to answer to a court-martial. Bloody Canadians. Bloody good soldiers, but they set their own rules. I suppose they are scattered all over on their leave?"

"Yes, sir. You'll probably find them in the lower class pubs and brothels of London and Paris."

"Yes, if any of them turn up AWOL when the leave is over, he will be our number one suspect. There is talk that the two companies in our charge are to be returned to the Canadian corps as their whole bloody army is being moved to our sector."

"Will that complicate the investigation, sir?"

"On the contrary, they will be lulled to complacency. The provost marshal will be working with his Canadian counterparts. It is conceivable that he will be asking you a few questions as well."

"Yes, sir," Captain Walker replied. "You'll have my fullest cooperation."

Chapter Sixteen

Paul and Chelsea caught the mid morning train to Dover and were soon heading across the countryside of southeast England. The train coach was filled with a noisy crowd of mostly families heading out for a Sunday outing, interspersed with a few soldiers heading home on leave.

As they entered the county of Kent, Paul observed that the countryside abounded in orchards. There were row upon row of neatly pruned apple, peach and pear trees dominating the countryside with their attendant quaint little farmsteads.

"So, where are the fields of clover?" Paul asked as they watched the orchards roll by.

"What?" Chelsea looked at him curiously.

"You know, like the song, 'We'll drive through fields of clover to the white cliffs of Dover on our golden wedding day.' You know, 'put on your old grey bonnet with the blue ribbon on it'" Paul laughed.

They both sang a verse from the old song and were joined by several others in the coach. After the song died down, Chelsea said in answer to his question, "It isn't our golden wedding day."

"Do we have to wait that long to see fields of clover?" Paul smiled.

"Look, we're coming up to Dover," Chelsea said excitedly as the train approached a small city that overlooked a seashore. To one side was a rise in the landscape near the edge of the sea.

"See the castle?" Chelsea said as she pointed to a great medieval fortress on the top of the rise. "That's Dover Castle. It's above the cliffs."

"Are we allowed to go near it?" Paul asked.

"Yes, it's open to the public. I'll take you there one day this week." Chelsea was elated at the prospect of showing Paul around Dover.

"Will you take me to the seashore, too?" Paul asked. "I've never properly been to a seashore other than to get on board a ship."

"Oh yes," Chelsea bubbled. "Right below the cliffs, perhaps we can even go swimming."

The train pulled into the Dover station and as they stepped out onto the station platform, Chelsea clasped Paul's hand and said, "Come on Paul darling, hail a cab and take us home."

"Your parents won't object to you suddenly showing up with a Canadian soldier on your arm?" Paul was apprehensive for the first time.

"I should think they won't. We have plenty of room. Of course we'll have to sleep in separate rooms."

"Of course," Paul replied. Then with a teasing voice added, "We wouldn't want them to think their daughter is a, what did you say, trollop?"

"Oh Paul, you're incorrigible," Chelsea scoffed.

They hailed a cab and it delivered them to a modest two-storey stone house just outside of Dover, near the edge of a small apple and cherry orchard.

"Your father is a horticulturist?" Paul asked as they stepped from the taxi.

"His home and orchard are part of an inheritance, my father is actually a postmaster."

"I hope I leave a good impression on your parents," Paul worried.

"Of course you will, just flash those innocent eyes at them. It will surely melt their hearts. My father was a military man who fought in the Boer War, so you'll have something in common with him."

"I surely hope so," was Paul's nervous reply.

Chelsea led Paul through the front gate to the front door. "Wait here. I'll announce you to my parents."

"Good idea," Paul replied anxiously as Chelsea went into the house.

As Paul stood at the door nervously kneading his hat that he held in his hands, a voice behind him said, "Are you waiting for someone to answer the door, young man?"

He turned and saw a middle-aged man wearing a tweed cap and jacket, sporting a thick mustache, standing behind him with a bag of, apparently, groceries in his hand and a newspaper tucked under his arm.

"Yes, Er. . . I am waiting for the young lady I am with to announce me," Paul replied.

"Chelsea?" He gave Paul a quizzical look.

"Yes, that's right."

"I am Chelsea's father," the man replied evenly.

"Pleased to meet you, sir," Paul replied stiffly, extending his hand.

"My pleasure, sir," Chelsea's father replied. "Did you escort her home then?"

"Yes, I came with her all the way from London."

"I say, that was decent of you, but by your manner of speech. . .?"

"I'm a Canadian, from Ontario."

"Well, I *am* delighted to meet you. You're the first Canadian I've ever met. I heard how you Canadian blokes stood your ground against the Hun when they first used the ruddy gas. Would you like to join us for tea?"

"I'd be delighted also, Mr. Pickford."

"To whom do I have the pleasure?"

"Paul Cunningham, sir."

"I am Alan Pickford. Shall we go in?"

Just then the door opened and Chelsea with her mother appeared.

"Oh Father!" she exclaimed as she threw herself into

his arms. "Jolly good to see you again."

"And this young man who escorted you home," her father chuckled.

"Oh Paul," Chelsea grinned as she turned to Paul. "I'd like you to meet my father."

"We've met," Paul laughed. "And he has invited me in for tea."

"Marvelous. Mother, this is Paul Cunningham from Canada."

"I'm terribly sorry it took so long to get to the door to let you in, but Chelsea had to tell me all about you."

"It's quite all right," Paul assured her. "It gave me an opportunity to meet Mr. Pickford."

"I trust there is more to this relationship than you merely escorting my daughter home," Alan chuckled.

"Oh yes, Father, much more."

"I see."

"Well, let's all go in and have tea, and you can tell me all about it."

They settled on padded chairs in a small living room in front of a fireplace, although the weather was much too warm to have a fire in the hearth. Chelsea sat on the arm of the chair where Paul sat, while her mother fussed about getting tea ready.

"So, have you been to the front?" Alan asked of Paul.

"Yes, I have been there since late June. This is my first furlough."

"I was in the Boer War you know and I have a son fighting the Turks in Mesopotamia[1]," Alan said proudly.

"He was married with a family when he ran off to fight in South Africa," Chelsea's mother scoffed as she brought through a tray with the tea service and a small

[1]Turkey, then known as the Ottoman Empire, was allied with Germany in WW1

dish of biscuits.

"Now, Mae," he said to Chelsea's mother, "her Majesty, Queen Victoria, was calling upon us to serve the Empire," Alan said with his English pride.

"Yes, I felt proud swearing an oath to His Majesty, King George V," Paul said.

"Yes, this ongoing scrap with the Hun has soldiers from all over the empire participating. Although they say Canada, Australia and New Zealand are independent Dominions now."

"Yes, I've seen soldiers from all over serving under the Union Jack."

"So, where on the front are you?"

"By the Somme."

"The Somme, yes the papers are full of accounts there. General Haig is confident he can break through the German lines there if he keeps up the pressure. It seems though, there have been a lot of casualties."

'A lot of casualties, is a gross understatement,' Paul thought. *'I wish I could tell him just how bad it really is.'*

"Let's talk about something else," Chelsea interjected. "Paul got his furlough to get away from the war. He only has ten days before he goes back."

"I agree," Mae added. "It's bad enough with all this ruddy rationing and the bloody Germans trying to starve us out."

"Perhaps I shouldn't stay here," Paul said quietly to Chelsea. "Your parents will be stretching their ration cards."

"Chelsea has invited Paul to stay with us over his furlough," Mae said to Alan. "She has time off from her entertaining also."

"I don't mean to impose," Paul said, his face flushed. "I know food is scarce with the rationing."

"Nonsense, we will make do," Alan replied firmly. "It will be a pleasure to put you up. A man in uniform is always welcome at this house."

"I insist on helping to pay for groceries. Sometimes servicemen can get around the rationing."

"That would be jolly good of you," Mae replied.

"So, have you known my daughter long?" Alan asked Paul.

"I met her when my regiment first arrived in England and we have been writing to each other while I was at the front," Paul replied.

"With incredible luck, his furlough coincided with my getting time off," Chelsea said. "Now, I will be able to show him the sights of Dover."

They dined on a skimpy supper, each being allotted a meat pie, a scoop of potatoes and a large spoonful of peas. After the main course, her mother put out a platter of fresh apples, cherries and peaches with the comment, "At least we have plenty of fruit this time of year. Feel free to eat as much as you like."

"So, does your family live right in Toronto?" Alan asked as they munched on dessert and her mother poured tea.

"Yes," Paul replied. "Right in the middle of the city."

"You said your father is a solicitor, did you not?" Chelsea added.

"Yes, we call his profession a lawyer over there."

"You must have money then," Mae said pleasantly. "Any solicitor I've ever heard of has loads of money."

"I'm surprised you're not an officer," Alan added.

"Yes, well. . . he wanted me to."

"Paul is uncomfortable talking about his family wealth," Chelsea interjected.

"We are not really wealthy," Paul said. "My father is comfortably well off, but I choose to make my own life. He felt I should be an officer or a noncombatant, but I had to prove myself by enlisting."

"That's very commendable," Mae added. "It is always the lot of ordinary folk to bear the burden, while the sons of rich men get cushy jobs away from the front."

"They used to taunt me as the rich kid at basic training, and my former tormentors, now my closest friends, still call me Rich Kid as a nickname," Paul replied. "Whether I become wealthy or live in poverty, after the war, it will be my choice not that of my father."

Sensing that there was a rift in Paul's family, Chelsea's parents asked no more about his family.

As Alan took another cherry from the bowel he asked, "Do they have orchards over in Canada?"

"Yes, there are orchards just outside of Toronto, in Nova Scotia and I believe, and away out west in British Columbia."

"I always thought Canada would be too ruddy cold," Chelsea added.

"Most of it is and even where I come from, which is one of the warmer areas, there is still a lot of snow."

"Oh yes, we get plenty of snow here also, on occasion." Alan added.

On the third day of his stay with Chelsea's family, they visited the great Dover Castle, a massive medieval fortification that loomed above the city of Dover. It was a fascinating structure with its turrets, battlements and an internal maze of corridors with portals and balconies that looked out upon the main hall. It was one of the few castles open to the public where one could have an almost free reign to explore the labyrinth-like passageways within.

At one point they came out on a high turret. It was a

cloudless day of crystal clarity. "Look, there's the coast of France," Chelsea said eagerly pointing southeastward at a vague bluish outline of land on the other side of the sea below them.

"Incredible, this narrow strait is all that separates heaven from hell," Paul replied. "It's hard to envision from here, that over there, men are dying by the hundreds every day."

"You must relax, Paul darling, enjoy your time on this side of the strait. Do you know that no army since the Battle of Hastings, nine hundred years ago, has ever set foot on our little island of freedom? Even Napoleon didn't know how to cross the strait."

Amazing," Paul replied. "The gates of hell opened for a little while to let me out to visit heaven, and it is heaven being here with you. Though all to soon, I'll have to return."

"Oh Paul, let's not talk about that now. Let's go down to the beach, where we won't have to see the shores of hell."

Later they walked along the sandy beach below the famed cliffs composed of white chalk limestone, though they bore a yellowish tinge from the passage of time.

"Feel better now that you can't see the shores of France?" Chelsea asked as they walked along swinging their arms that were joined by their tightly clutched hands. In the background was the rushing sounds of breakers lapping the shore and the cry of the ever-present gulls overhead.

"Much better," Paul smiled. He noted that the coast of France was invisible from the seashore. Then looking at the sky, he suddenly cried, "What's that!"

"Oh no, not another Zeppelin," Chelsea cried at the sight of a giant cigar-shaped German airship heading inland. "It's heading for London to drop some bombs."

"I thought you said England was safe from invaders," Paul said.

"These Zeppelins are more of a nuisance than a threat," Chelsea assured him. "The Germans are so desperate, they not only are trying to starve us out with their ruddy submarines, but they bombard us with blimps."

"I've heard of these so-called Zeppelins, but this is the first time I've seen one."

"So are you enjoying the seashore," Chelsea said deliberately changing the subject.

"Yes, it is sort of exhilarating, nothing to hear except the sounds of the sea and the gulls."

"You say you came from a well-to-do family, but never spent time on the seashore?" Chelsea asked.

"I guess a seaside vacation wasn't in my parents' plans," Paul replied. "I remember once having a brief visit to the seashore when we went to Boston and of course during the time we went to England when I was a child. I've been to the shore of Lake Ontario lots in remote areas outside the city. Lake Ontario is so large that you can't see the other side. Even though there are plenty of gulls around, it isn't quite like the seashore."

"Tell me, Paul, do you really dislike your family."

"No, I don't dislike them. My mother is from a wealthy family, and my father aspires to be wealthy and connected. He has always tried to direct my life as he does the life of my sisters. He wants us to marry into the right families and set our sights high."

"And you don't want to set your sights high?"

"However I set my sights, I want to be the one aiming. I want to choose my own life, whether wealthy or poor and to choose my own wife. He didn't want me to join up and if I must join up, he expected me to become an officer, like the other so-called rich kids."

"And your two sisters?"

Paul smiled for a moment and continued, "They are both younger than me. Victoria, or Vicky as we call her, is the youngest and is a trifle spoiled, but she is only twelve years old. Then there is Ginny."

"Ginny, as in Virginia?" Chelsea asked.

"Yes," Paul smiled. "She is not only my sister, but my confident who shares the secrets of my soul. I told her all about you."

"And?"

"She is anxious to meet you. You'd like her. She is a beautiful person and so mature for one who is only sixteen."

"What would your parents say if they knew you were going about with the daughter of a postmaster, and a common entertainer?"

"They'd be shocked of course. But it doesn't matter what they think. Ginny would welcome you with open arms."

"What are you saying, Paul," Chelsea said, stopping and looking up at him. Then with a wry grin she added, "It seems that you are getting presumptuous again."

In a burst of courage Paul said, "Will you marry me, Chelsea? When this war is over, I will take you home to Canada." He grabbed her and kissed her.

"Oh, Paul, I don't know what to say," Chelsea gasped with her cheek on his.

"Just say yes. We can wait for my next furlough and plan a proper wedding."

"Oh, Paul, you barge into my life and steal my heart with those innocent eyes of yours and now you want me to marry you. I don't know what to say."

"Just say yes, that is unless you don't love me."

"Oh, Paul. Of course I love you, but you are a little

overwhelming at times."

"Okay, we can talk about it later."

"But don't say anything to my parents until I give a definite yes," Chelsea said.

"I promise, but it will be a hard secret to bear, while you torture me with suspense."

"I'll try not to torture you too long," Chelsea grinned as she leaned up and kissed him

That evening when they returned to Chelsea's parents' place, a letter was waiting for Chelsea. It was from her employer. She tore into it anxiously and her face grew serious as she read it.

> *Dear Chelsea,*
>
> *I trust you are enjoying your vacation with your family and the young soldier. I hate to be one to burst a bubble and bring you back to reality, but I have some exciting news about the future of our little troupe. We have an engagement at the Royal Music Hall, where there are bound to be members of royalty in attendance. If you leave a good impression with that marvelous voice of yours, you may even get to sing before the King. Can you imagine performing in front of His Majesty. As it is, we definitely have an engagement in Paris later this year and some performances for the boys at the front. With all of this under our belts we are bound to go to New York after the war. I would like to ask you to return early so we can begin rehearsal for that all-important engagement at the Royal Music Hall.*
>
> *Sincerely Yours*
> *Chas.*

"I must go to my room for a while," Chelsea said to Paul upon reading the letter. Her head was crashing with conflicting emotions and desires.

"The news is that disquieting?" Paul replied. "Perhaps you'd like to share it with me."

"Perhaps later," Chelsea replied. She turned and headed for her room.

She lay in her room clutching the letter with the conflicting visions of the young innocent-looking Paul asking her to marry him, and the words of Chas saying, *"You are twenty-two and you want to throw your life away for a ruddy young pup of a soldier who will probably leave you a widow before this war is over."* His gilded words offering her a promising future as a great entertainer where she could become famous was offset with concerns that she might be rejected by Paul's family and he in turn ostracized by them. Canada could be a big lonely place. Oh, what should she do?

Paul looked puzzled at what could have upset Chelsea.

"It's from her employer," Mae replied.

"He didn't fire her, did he?"

"I don't know."

Later when Chelsea emerged for supper, she seemed somewhat distant, but Paul did convince her to go for a walk through the orchard. He hoped to find out what was troubling her.

"Did he fire you for taking too long on your vacation?" Paul asked as they walked along under the apple trees.

"Don't be silly," she snapped. "Then in a more temperate voice she continued, "It was quite the contrary. He offered me a chance to sing before the King and to go to Paris."

"Is that something to be upset about?"

"You don't understand." She gave Paul a pleading look.

"I only understand that I love you and I presume you love me." Paul gave her his innocent eyes.

"There you go with those eyes again," Chelsea chided. "You don't understand. I have a chance to become a star. That is no mean task for a woman you know."

"So, go and sing before the King or go to Paris, you'll have plenty of time before my next furlough. In between engagements, you can plan our wedding." He caught Chelsea by the arm and looked her in the eye. "I do love you and I want to marry you. Please say yes?"

"Oh Paul, you're impossible." Chelsea slowly leaned into him.

They kissed briefly and Chelsea drew away saying, "I promise I will give you your answer in the morning."

"I won't sleep a wink waiting to hear it," Paul grinned.

Although they walked back to the house, arm in arm, Paul could feel a certain distance about her.

Paul spent a fitful night tossing and turning as he tried to fathom why a seemingly simple request was so complex for Chelsea to answer. When he did finally fall asleep, he slept longer than usual the following morning. He came awake suddenly with the sun streaming in on his face, realizing it was quite late. He sprang out of bed, dressed and hurried downstairs. Today was the day that Chelsea was to end the suspense and presumably accept his proposal.

"Is Chelsea up yet?" Paul asked her mother as he came into the living room.

"She's been up for some time," Mae said gravely. "Our daughter is a coward." She handed Paul a letter. Paul swallowed as he sat down to read it, fearing the worst.

Dear Paul,

You will think me a coward for running away, but I could not bear to look into those innocent eyes of yours and tell you that I cannot accept your proposal of marriage. I have a chance to become a major star, with opportunities not only to sing before royalty, but to travel to Paris, and after the war is over, to New York and beyond. Opportunities for a woman are limited and I must not miss this chance.

I, as the daughter of a mere postmaster and a common entertainer, would not fit well in your family. They would probably look down upon me as from a lower station and scorn me for keeping you from marrying within your own station. You may say that their opinion doesn't matter, but you are young and full of defiance. Estrangement from your family can be a bitter pill that can last a long, long time. I wish you well in your hopes and dreams and pray to God that you survive this terrible war in good form.

If you cannot forgive me for running out on you, I will understand. I will always love you and hold the wonderful times we had together dear to my heart forever more. God Bless You and keep you safe at the front.

Love

Chelsea

Paul's heart sank and his stomach fell as he folded the letter and put it in his tunic pocket. He had no desire to eat the breakfast Chelsea's mother had offered, though he did accept a cup of tea.

"She left this morning?" Paul asked morosely.

"She caught the early train to London," Mae said sadly. "She said to tell you not to follow her back to London. Although she was crying, she said she did not want to become either a war widow or an outcast in a wealthy family."

Paul looked glumly at her, silently cursing his father for making such an issue of being wealthy.

"I'm so sorry, young man," she said with sympathy. "I am sure you would have made a good husband for Chelsea."

"Is there a ferry from here across to France?" Paul asked.

"Yes, I believe there is. It transports a lot of military supplies."

"Well, I'm military supplies," Paul said in a downcast tone.

Chapter Seventeen

It was with heavy heart that Paul boarded the ferry from Dover to Calais. He was sailing back into hell, somehow feeling that he had been cast out of heaven with Chelsea's rejection of his hand. He was ready to fight the Hun now as he felt that all the tenderness of life had been wrenched from him. Most of the passengers on the boat were servicemen like himself, returning to duty at the front. Bob was not among them as he would be catching the boat from Portsmouth to LeHavre thinking that he, Paul, went AWOL for the love of Chelsea. '*What a laugh that is,*' Paul thought bitterly. It was just as well. He wasn't ready to face his friends yet.

From Calais, Paul caught a troop train to Ameins. This French city located near the front served as a major supply centre and local command headquarters. At this major base camp just outside of the city, which served as a repository for military supplies, he found a new curious weapon of war being unloaded from flatcars. They were strange iron vehicles with motors at the rear and a set of endless tracks for propulsion going up and over each side. Out each side of these contrivances was a small cupola fitted with a machine-gun. This was the latest weapon of warfare, the battle tank. Paul watched them sputter and clank along at a snail's pace belching evil smelling black smoke from their exhausts. They were forever stalling as they moved into their assembly area.

Paul stopped beside one of the stalled tanks for a closer look at these strange-looking machines. He was startled at the voices of two other soldiers who came alongside him.

"Dae ye think these mechanical contraptions will

win thae war, Angus?" one of them said to the other with a broad Scottish brogue.

"I canna say, Malcolm, ye never know whah these bloody Englishmen will come wi next," Angus replied with a chuckle

Paul turned and was awed by the sight of the two Scottish soldiers that stood beside him. They were tall and fair complected. Their expressions were firm set and dour, reflecting the fierce pride of their race. They wore standard army tunics, but their caps were different with a tassel on top and below the tunic they wore kilts with the tartan of their regiment. These proud people, warriors and explorers alike, to whom defeat or admission of failure was an alien concept, had charted unknown continents and claimed half a planet for their king and country. When battle was called for, they were there, marching fearlessly in the face of death to the shrill music of their bagpipes.

"What dae ye think ae these mechanical monsters, laddie?" Angus asked Paul.

"I don't know sir," Paul said in a timid voice. "I hope they win the war for us, sir."

"There's nae need tae call me sir, laddie," Angus laughed. "We're noh officers."

"Yes, sir," Paul replied. He couldn't help but address these professional warriors as sir, even if they were from the enlisted ranks.

"I think I'll still put my faith in my rifle and bayonet," Malcolm added. "Thae Englishmen can have these mechanical beasties."

"Aye," Angus replied.

"They don't seem to work very well," Paul observed

"Aye, the German cannons will blow these things tae smithereens," Malcolm agreed.

"We better gae noo, and try tae catch a lorry back tae

our place at thae front," Angus said.

"Aye, well good luck in fightin' thae Hun, laddie," Malcolm said to Paul as they turned and walked away.

'*God help the Germans that tangle with their regiment,*' Paul thought as he watched the kilt-clad warriors walk away. '*The Scots were right.*' He would rather put his faith in the cannons, at least he knew they worked. Paul thought he should also catch a ride on one of the trucks, or lorries as the Scots called them, out to his company headquarters.

Paul arrived at the motor pool area and presented his ID to the guard on duty.

"North Ontario Regiment, I say, that's a Canadian outfit," the guard said.

"Yes it is, but B & C companies are on loan to the South London regiment."

"I am told that I must send any Canadian soldiers to the west camp as the whole corps is being assembled there."

"The whole Canadian corps?"

"Yes, I understand that the entire Canadian Army is being reassigned to fight in the Somme sector."

"Excellent, we get to go back to our own army," Paul grinned. This also meant that he'd be away from the English regiment in case of any lingering doubts about Lieutenant Bedford's death.

*   *   *

Captain Walker was again summoned to regimental headquarters to the office of Colonel Wilson. In attendance at the meeting was also the provost marshal.

"I will get directly to the point," Wilson said as all were seated. "We have definite reason to believe there was foul play concerning the death of Lieutenant Bedford. So the provost marshal would like to ask a few questions."

"How did you come to this conclusion, sir, if I may ask?" Walker asked.

"Well, like you said, the bullet hole in the head was too small for a Mauser. We had the bullet extracted from his brain and ballistics have determined that it was from his own revolver. One that had two shots fired from it."

"But only one in his head."

"The point is, one of them did hit him in the head and it killed him."

"But the pistol was in his hand when they brought him in, sir," Walker insisted. "Could he have committed suicide."

"It is possible, but unlikely," Wilson continued.

"The stretcher-bearers say he was all covered with mud from head to toe," the provost marshal interjected. "This implies a struggle."

"Indeed," Walker replied.

"So, Captain Walker," the provost marshal continued, "did you observe any other soldiers covered with mud, that day?"

Walker thought and recalled the soldier who had escorted the prisoner in. He was suspicious at the time, but discarded the suspicions after the interview and wrote Bedford off as merely another casualty. Now that the matter was blown open, he would have to tell all to save his career.

After a moment he replied, "Yes there was another soldier, Lance Corporal Cunningham, who brought a prisoner in just before Bedford was brought in. He was also covered in mud."

"Interesting. Were the others, including the prisoner, also quite muddy?"

"Not that muddy. Mostly they had muddy feet. These two looked like they had rolled in the mud."

"Why didn't you mention this before, Captain?" Wilson demanded

"Well, I suppose, sir, I assumed that Bedford was killed by enemy fire. Usually bad officers are shot in the back, if their own men kill them."

"But there was obviously a struggle," Wilson added.

"It looked that way and I did interview Cunningham that evening looking for clues."

"And," the provost marshal persisted. "He betrayed no overt signs of guilt or otherwise trying to hide something."

"You assumed he was not guilty then?"

"Yes, sir. If I had thought he was guilty I would have turned him in."

"I see. I trust he denied witnessing the Lieutenant's death?"

"Yes, sir."

"Didn't you think it odd that they were the only ones covered with mud."

"Yes. And that is why I interviewed him. Also, I assumed the lieutenant probably fell into the mud when he was hit. Cunningham said he was pushed into the mud by a German soldier that fell on top of him."

"You should have told us all of this earlier, Captain, instead of making assumptions," Wilson said sharply. "Consider yourself on report."

"Yes, sir."

"I should like to interview this prisoner," the provost marshal said. "I somehow think he is at the centre of this whole matter."

"It shouldn't be too much trouble to track down which POW camp is holding him."

"As for you, Captain, you can start redeeming yourself by finding out if any of these Canadians from

Company C are AWOL. Now that they are back with their own army, you'll have to contact their CO," Wilson said.

"Yes, sir."

"Good idea," the provost marshal said. "We'll want to keep this investigation as low profile as possible, until we are ready to make an arrest."

*   *   *

Paul had scarcely entered the Canadian sector of the camp when he was hailed by a familiar voice. It was Curtis. Bob and Dale were with him.

"Hey how are you?" Curtis slapped him on the back. "You didn't get married or something foolish like that while you were in England?"

"No, nothing foolish like that," Paul said in a low voice.

"Something is wrong. Did you and your lady friend have a fight?"Curtis continued.

"Yeah, it's all over."

"Too bad, buddy."

"I told you she'd dump you." Dale, who had an uncommon knack for speaking out of line, chimed in. "You were just one of many."

Paul's fist shot out and Dale was left sprawling on the ground. "I'll thank you to keep your mouth shut, Runt," Paul rumbled.

"Wow, sensitive aren't we?" Bob added.

"It's probably best we don't talk about Chelsea for awhile," Curtis said as Dale crawled to his feet nursing a tender jaw. To Paul he said warmly, "When you're ready to talk about it, buddy, I'll listen."

"So, I understand we are rejoining our own army again," Paul said, deliberately changing the subject.

"Yeah, our whole division came to the Somme sector," Curtis replied. "There's something big gonna happen soon."

"Yeah, I guess they want some real soldiers to take part," Bob laughed. "So they called for Canadians."

"We'll have our own officers again," Paul said. "That's a relief."

"Yeah, for you I am sure," Curtis said. "Though we are still under British generals."

"With all of our army in one place, we'll really hit the Hun between the horns," Dale added.

"I see some Scottish units about," Paul added. "Two of their soldiers spoke to me when I was looking at the tanks."

"With them and the Canadians together, the Hun doesn't have a chance," Bob added.

"Let's go over to the canteen and get some sweets to take back to our bunks," Bob said to Dale. Dale agreed and they left Paul and Curtis to go on alone.

Paul and Curtis continued to walk toward their billets in silence until Paul finally spoke. "You were probably right," he said bitterly. "A whore is a soldier's best friend. At least there are no attachments."

"No, buddy, you were right and I was wrong. If you've seen one whorehouse, you've seen them all. I've been in brothels in London, in Paris and even Toronto. They're all the same and serve only one purpose. They do a trick for a bob or a franc, or whatever currency is at hand. Cigarettes are a universal currency. No Paul, you had love. You don't get that with painted ladies."

"The key word here is 'had,'" Paul said despondently. "I thought I had love, but I had an illusion."

"Did she jilt you that badly?" Curtis asked with understanding.

"Yes. She is a wonderful singer who was offered a

career with her voice," he laughed bitterly and continued, "She might even get to sing before the King."

"She was offered gold so she dumped you for it?" Curtis asked..

"Who could fault her? It is not often that a woman can get to be famous," Paul said. "I hold no bitterness toward her."

"That's good! There is enough bitterness in the hell we find ourselves in without an aching heart."

"Yeah," Paul sighed.

"Well, time heals and if these new so-called battle tanks work, the war will be over soon and we'll all go home."

"Do you think those mechanical contraptions will work?" Paul scoffed. "The way they sputter and cough I'd rather put my faith in my rifle."

"Well, we can always hope they'll make the difference. We can't seem to break through the German lines any other way."

"Yeah," Paul replied without inflection as he drew another cigarette.

As they reached their billet consisting of one of those round tents that could house their squad, Curtis said, "Why don't you write that sister of yours, Ginny, is it? She always cheers you up."

"Ah yes, Ginny," Paul smiled. "I'll need to tell her it's all over with Chelsea."

"There, that's better," Curtis said as he placed a hand on Paul's back.

"You're a real friend and confidant," Paul said. "More than any rich kid could ask for."

"It's okay, Rich Kid, we'll pull through this war together." Curtis put his hand on Paul's shoulder.

"When it's over, I'll take you to Toronto with me. I'd love to introduce you to Ginny."

"She sounds like a very special person, by the way you describe her," Curtis smiled.

"She is more special than I could ever describe," Paul reiterated as they entered the billet. "Did they bring all our stuff here from the front?"

"Yeah, it all came in one big pile," Curtis replied. "We sorted your things out along with ours."

"Thanks, Pal"

Once inside, since they still had a few hours till 'lights out,' Paul fished his writing pad out of his kit bag. On the inside front cover of the pad he kept a picture of Ginny. There was also one of Chelsea laying on top of it. Paul winced at the sight of her and quickly put the picture of Chelsea in the bottom of his kit bag where he wouldn't have to see it. He came over to where Curtis was lying on his bunk and with the picture in hand he said, "This is a picture of Ginny."

"Wow, she's a real looker," Curtis said at the sight of the strikingly attractive girl in her youth with her long flowing hair.

"The best part of her beauty lies within her," Paul replied.

"I'd like to meet her one day," Curtis said, "but she'd probably look down on a poor son of a railway worker from Winnipeg."

"Not Ginny," Paul laughed as he went back to his bunk to start the letter, "she'd judge you for who you are as a person, not by your social standing. My parents on the other hand. . ."

Paul began his letter:

Dear Ginny,
It is with heavy heart that I tell you that it is all over
for Chelsea and me. We spent a wonderful week to-
gether at her parents' home in Dover while I was on

furlough. When I proposed marriage to her, she first hesitated then rejected me in favour of her career. She is also worried that I'll be killed and leave her a widow. However, I did make the same promise to her as I did to you. I will return. Now that it is over, you won't have to ever mention the affair to Mom and Dad. They in turn will not have to be concerned that their son is marrying below his station, at least for the foreseeable future.

Just then, Bob and Dale entered the tent. Paul put a blotter over his letter.

"Writing kiss and make up letters are we?" Dale ventured.

"I'm writing a letter home," Paul said through gritted teeth.

"Leave him be," Curtis said. "Or are you trying to get out of trench duty by getting a broken jaw?"

Dale settled down on his own bunk while Paul opened his pad and resumed writing his letter to his sister. He dearly wished that he could speak personally with Ginny about his aching heart.

Chapter Eighteen

The following morning, the Canadian contingent for the Somme sector, also called the Byng Boys in reference to their overall commander General Sir Jullian Byng, was assembled in company sized groups, with Company C once again getting Canadian officers.

"I am your new CO, Captain Robbins," the captain said to C Company. He then introduced his four commanding lieutenants, the one for Paul's platoon being Lieutenant Palmer. The captain then went on to explain, "The division is to get a whole section of the front, including their own artillery and some of the tanks. We are to be placed in a segment of the front facing the village of Courcelette. Both the village and a nearby defense bastion known as the Sugar Factory, held by the Germans, will be our objective when the offensive gets underway. We will now board trucks to deliver us to our quarters at the front. They are to be evacuated by some English regiments in order to make way for us."

Later as the corps was moving into its new position, a Zeppelin appeared in the sky far above them, slowly and silently gliding overhead spying on their movements. As they were setting up artillery and moving men into the front trenches, the Zeppelin dropped a few small bombs. "Duck for cover!" was the cry. The bombs exploded, wrecking one cannon and inflicting several casualties.

"Too bad that overgrown balloon is so far up in the sky," Paul said. "I'd shoot it down."

Just then, two British airplanes appeared. As they closed in on the blimp, one of them was shot down by the crew on board. The other airplane managed to fire into the dirigible igniting its hydrogen filled interior. The Zeppelin went up in one gigantic fireball and crashed to earth behind the lines.

It must have gotten a signal off to the ground forces, for almost immediately afterward, the German cannons began a savage bombardment of the front Canadian trenches.

"Fall back," came the cry as Canadian soldiers scrambled away from the incoming artillery shells. Though not soon enough as bodies, several at a time, were hurtled upward with each exploding shell. Soon Canadian artillery returned fire in a carpet of shelling on the German lines. Bodies could be observed leaping upward from that quarter also. The murderous duel raged for several hours as Paul and his buddies hunkered down in their trenches, weathering a constant rain of debris, and occasional body parts, praying that they would not be a victim of a direct hit. The artillery died down after a time and the cry went out for, "Over the top."

The soldiers of Paul's company and one other company, sprang out of their trenches and charged headlong. The Germans were given the same order and the two armies collided in the middle of no-mans-land like linebackers in a rugby game. They bayoneted and shot each other with homicidal fury until a few pathetic survivors from each side finally crawled back to their own trenches.

Roll call the next morning told a sad tale. The supposed main offensive had not even gotten underway and already the division had sustained twenty-six hundred casualties. Paul's squad had sustained three casualties with one dead. Their company as a whole, lost thirteen men. As that segment of the front quieted down, Paul looked out accross no-man's-land at the scattered bodies from both armies. They were told there would be no body recovery, as they would be soon going on the attack and all of the dead would be dealt with then.

On the evening of September 14, the artillery began a ferocious barrage upon the German trenches and kept up an all-night barrage. As the wind was favourable, some of the shells contained phosgene gas. In the rear, rows of clanking, sputtering, and rattling battle tanks were brought up for battle. In the wee hours just before sunrise, soldiers, including those of Paul's unit, were briefed about the impending offensive.

Their CO told them, "Our objectives today are the Sugar Factory and Courcelette. The infantry will follow slowly behind the tanks. A new technique called creeping artillery barrages will be used to keep the enemy off balance"

They were then given a sermon by the chaplain and issued a grog of strong rum to ready them for battle, and then they were sent to the front trenches. As the tanks all lined up to lead the attack, many of them sputtered and stalled. Mechanics scrambled to try to get them going again. At daybreak the cannons stopped, save for those laying down a line of fire along the German front lines. Those tanks that were still running were sent forward, rattling along, crawling over shell craters and trench works. In the latter case, makeshift bridges had been set up to accommodate the tanks. Some dropped into the trenches, missing or breaking the bridge, and got stuck. Infantrymen, including Paul, walked slowly behind the tanks ready to storm the German trenches, while the gunners within the tanks fired bursts from their machine-guns at the German positions.

German artillery soon zeroed in on some of the tanks turning them into exploding fireballs, cremating the crews within. Nonetheless, many of the tanks were able to reach the German trenches forcing a general retreat in some areas. As the Canadians reached the front German trenches, now largely evacuated, the cannons were either moved or their trajectory adjusted so the line of fire would move forward according to the creeping artillery barrage tactic. Thus the Germans were kept off balance and confused. By eight o'clock that morning, the Sugar Factory defense complex had been captured by the Canadians and dozens of German prisoners were taken.

The fighting was ferocious as the retreating Germans were making their opponents pay in blood for every step of the way. They even managed a few small-scale counter-offensives to try to slow the Canadians down. In this mad world of shooting and stabbing, human cries of anguish were drowned out by the roar of machine-guns and exploding artillery shells. Paul and his friends slogged on more like zombies than living human beings as day turned into night and back into day again. The world seemed to fade into an awful twilight of grey with the sky lit by dozens of cannon muzzles on both sides. Whenever the wind turned against them, they had to quickly don their gas masks as the Germans would flood them with both chlorine and phosgene. When the wind shifted in their favour, blowing the gas back at the Germans, they would release their own canisters of gas. Wearing gas gear was hellish as it was hot and suffocating under the masks with the eye pieces often fogging up making it impossible to see. In the midst of it all, Paul could think of only two things, survival and kill or be killed.

By the end of the fourth day, the front had moved forward up to four miles in some areas. The village of Courcelette, now reduced to a smouldering ruin by cannon fire from both sides, was now behind them. Frightened civilians emerged from shattered homes to stare blankly at the Khaki-clad soldiers moving among them supposedly from a friendly army. However, by this time most of the tanks had either been destroyed or suffered mechanical breakdown and rearguard German artillery began to take its toll on the infantry despite the creeping barrages. The Germans were holed up in a former wooded area now reduced to a tangle of broken trees, looking as if a tornado had struck the area. The fallen trees made excellent shelter for the defenders and the Canadians could advance no more as machine gun nests and field cannons within the tangle of trees, mowed down any who tried. Thus, they had to dig in once again. Everywhere the battlefield was littered with bodies from both armies. The smell of death hung in the air as no one had time to collect the dead and some bodies were starting to decompose turning a sickly green in colour. Others attracted swarms of large ugly rats with greasy-looking fur, greasy from a constant diet of rotting flesh. They competed with the flies for the abundant corpses on hand. No matter how many men fell from bullets, cannon shells or gas, the rat population never seemed to dwindle. If anything they thrived on death. In this surreal world of death and living hell, the Grim Reaper chose no favourites. Paul oddly observed that dead German soldiers carried the same sickly odour and colour as did their Canadian counterparts.

The all-clear was sounded, indicating that it was safe to take off their respirators. The battle sounds had died down to a few sporadic artillery duels. The platoon to which Paul belonged secured a drainage ditch to hole up in and they quickly got out their trenching spades to make the ditch deeper and wider. Machine gunners scrambled to secure their positions, and sandbags were brought up to protect them, pushed into place from behind. Curtis was busy directing the men around him as the sergeant was nowhere about. Finally the men of Company C paused to catch their breath.

Paul wiped his sopping face with a dirty hanky that he kept in his trouser pocket as he paused in his digging, and complained, "God, I hope they don't use any more gas for a while, I just about suffocated under that mask."

"Yeah, I couldn't see where I was going half the time," Curtis replied as he lit a cigarette.

"Has anybody seen Bob?" Dale asked as he came up alongside Curtis.

"I haven't seen him since the last gas attack," Paul replied.

"Yeah, with the mask on, you can't tell who is who," Curtis added.

"You don't suppose. . ?" Dale said apprehensively.

"I hope not," Curtis said, swallowing at the thought that his friend could have been killed.

"The sergeant will do a head count soon," Paul added with calm assurance. "Everything is so tangled up, he could be anywhere."

"The sergeant is dead," Dale said flatly. "I saw his body a while ago. His guts were all spilled out."

Paul winced at the thought, in spite of all the carnage he had seen these past few days. He tried not to think that Bob may have met the same fate.

"Okay, everyone," Curtis said to all within earshot. "Let's get this trench shored up and hopefully they'll bring up some ammo."

Presently Lieutenant Palmer appeared; he was limping and one arm was in a sling with his fore arm completely bandaged up. By this time a lateral trench had been dug to connect to the next row behind them.

"Corporal Smith," he said to Curtis.

"Sir," Curtis saluted.

"Since your sergeant is dead, and you show leadership qualities, I am authorized to promote you to staff sergeant and squad commander effective immediately. Lance Corporal Cunningham, you are promoted to full corporal and your first duty is to do a head count of surviving members of your squad."

"Yes, sir," Paul replied.

"We will be holding this position until further notice as we don't think the Hun is in any better position to attack than we are. All others, at your posts and continue digging in. I will try to send up more ammo for the machine-guns."

"Yes, sir," came the ripple of reply from the other soldiers in the area.

"You may use your iron rations from your packs, but eat sparingly. I can't say when the field kitchen will be moved up, but it will be as soon as possible."

"Oh joy, bully beef," Dale grumbled, as this tinned prepared meat was the standard of their so-called iron rations. As if eating tinned meat that might have passed for dog food in a normal world and rock-hard biscuits wasn't bad enough, a storm came up that evening. The storm turned into a a three day downpour that left their world of freshly churned up earth a horrible quagmire. The drainage ditch that they had widened and deepened for their defensive position served its original intent better than ever. Soon a stream was rushing through it leaving them knee-deep in muck.

*   *   *

At a PoW camp in Wales, Kurt Schmidt was summoned to the commandant's headquarters where an investigator for the provost marshal waited to interview him. As he approached the seated officer, he saluted respectfully.

"Sprechen Sie Englisch?" the officer asked.

"*Jawohl Herr Hauptmann*," Kurt replied smartly, though he was uncertain of the officer's rank.

"Since you can speak English, this interview will be conducted exclusively in English. "Is that clear, soldier."

"*Jawohl*, I mean yes, sir."

"Please be seated then," the officer said blandly.

Kurt sat uneasily at the edge of his chair, wondering as to the purpose of this interview.

"You are Private Kurt Schmidt of the first Hamburg regiment?"

"Yes, sir."

"On August 17, your unit conducted an attack on the British Army in the central Somme sector."

"Yes, sir, ve vhere ordered to."

"I am sure you were," the officer continued in his quiet almost pleasant voice. "In the course of your attack you found yourself trapped in a trench in no-man's-land with two Canadian soldiers, did you not?"

"Yes, sir," Kurt swallowed. He now knew why he had been called in.

"You were wounded in the shoulder and one of them treated your wound. His name was . .?"

"His name vas Paul. He vas very kind, but ve treat English soldiers zhat fall in our hands very *gut, Ja*."

"Just answer the questions please. The other soldier with him was Curtis Smith."

"*Ja*, zhat's right."

"Later the tommies recaptured that trench and the platoon leader Lieutenant Bedford appeared."

Kurt swallowed hard. *'They know about the incident. Someone must have squealed.'*

"What happened when the Lieutenant came?" the officer continued relentlessly.

"I don't remember." Kurt did not want to say anything that would reflect badly on his two kindly Canadian captors. "It vas a vhile ago."

"Is three weeks a long time?"

"I don't know. Do I have to answer zese questions?"

"Yes you do. We believe that the lieutenant was murdered."

Kurt swallowed hard and his eyes darted about.

"Why did Lance Corporal Paul Cunningham murder his lieutenant? Or was it Corporal Smith?"

"It vas not *Schmidt*," Kurt blundered.

"Then it was Cunningham. Why did he murder the lieutenant?" the officer demanded.

"It vas accident. Zhere vas no murder," Kurt suddenly blurted.

"Ah huh, it was an accident. Suppose you tell us about it, now that your memory seems to have recovered."

Kurt was silent as he assessed his blunder.

"I suggest you tell us everything. It is a long way from here to your home in Hamburg."

"You cannot zhreaten me, I haff *mein* rights, unter ze Geneva convention."

The officer laughed and said, "The Geneva convention exists at the convenience of the signers. I think you know that. You could easily be shot trying to escape, if you know what I mean."

"*Jawohl*, yes, sir," Kurt replied with bowed head. He was at their mercy, and since they seemed to know about the incident, it would probably go better for Paul if he told all."

"Okay I vill tell. Mit all due respect, ze Lieutenant vas a mad man. He vas going to kill me und Paul Cunningham."

"A mad man? Please explain."

Kurt then related the whole story as the officer

listened intently and his stenographer recorded Kurt's statement.

"Do you, Kurt Schmidt, swear before Almighty God, that you have told the whole truth in this statement?"

"I swear before *mein Gott* und all zhat ist holy, zhat I haff spoken ze truth."

"Thank you for your cooperation," the investigator said. "You may return to barracks."

"Vill zhey shoot Paul Cunningham?" asked a concerned Kurt.

"I don't know. That will be for a court-martial to decide. You are dismissed, prisoner"

*   *   *

Bob was not among the members of their squad still at the front line and with sinking heart, Paul soon discovered that he was also not among the wounded at the rear. Over the next few days as the bodies were collected from the battlefield, his dog tag number was compared to those taken from the dead, but no match could be found. Finally when all the identified dead were accounted for, Paul presented his list to the lieutenant. Their squad of twelve men had three confirmed killed including the sergeant and two wounded. Bob was unaccounted for.

"Lance Corporal Robert White will be declared as missing in action," was the Lieutenant Palmer's frank reply.

"Is that all, sir?" Paul replied. "Just declared as missing, no more search?"

"What do you want me to say, corporal, dig up no-man's-land until we find his body?"

"Is that where you think he is sir?" Paul asked in a small voice.

"He is either buried in the rubble, blown to smithereens, or taken prisoner by the Hun," the lieutenant said bluntly.

Paul swallowed but said nothing.

"Was he a friend of yours?" the lieutenant asked in a more tender voice.

"Yes, sir."

"Then for your sake, I hope he has been taken prisoner."

"I hope so, sir. Is there any way of finding out?"

"By the Geneva Convention, the German High Command is required to list all POWs with the Red Cross."

"We can find out from the Red Cross if he has been taken captive, sir?"

"Regimental HQ will be notified. I will watch for his name and let you know."

"Thank you, sir." Paul saluted.

"Do a good job of looking after that squad and I'll make you a sergeant one day also," the lieutenant said without inflection."

"Thank you, sir."

"Dismissed, Corporal."

"Yes, sir."

Two weeks later they were informed that Bob had indeed been taken prisoner. He was held in a compound called Stalag 13, deep inside Germany. Paul thought of the German prisoner whose wounds he had dressed. He could only hope that Bob's captors would show the same compassion.

After two more weeks of ferocious fighting, both repelling counterattacks and trying to storm the German trenches, German lines proved again to be too difficult to break through. The new trench works were expanded to take on a more permanent stance once again. The body count was appalling and the cycle was endless.

Chapter Nineteen
October 1916

Reveille came all too early as Paul and the others scrambled out of their bunks to quickly put on their uniforms. Paul's was still damp from yesterday's rain. The squad assembled and Curtis, in his roll as sergeant, did his usual quick inspection, looking for facial stubble and ill-kept gear. Satisfied that all was well, they were dismissed for breakfast. It was the beginning of probably another dreary day in the trenches. Paul hoped it would be uneventful, that is, neither his outfit being sent over the top or having to fend off the Hun being sent over the top. Though they were on rest time, they could be called back to the front line in a moment. The artillery was still blasting away and as they ate, trucks were bringing up more ammo. There were even a few extra cannons being brought forward by teams of horses.

"They're getting ready for something," Curtis remarked as they watched the procession go by. Even though he was promoted to sergeant, he still retained personal friendship with Paul as a corporal, and Dale who was now a lance corporal.

Captain Robbins came to the mess tent and everyone rose to attention. "At ease, soldiers," he said. "You may be seated."

When everyone sat back down, he resumed, "All of C company is being granted a twenty-four hour leave in Albert. Since it is a short leave, you won't have time to go to Ameins"

A cheer rippled through the company and Paul said to Curtis, "For sure we are going over the top tomorrow."

"Our company has fought long and hard, and we deserve a break. You may catch a ride into town with the ammo trucks, once they have unloaded. Your sergeants will issue passes and will do a head count when the trucks assemble to bring you home at midnight. This is not necessarily a prelude to an attack, so please don't even speculate such while in town. Any speculation, true or false, plays into the hands of the Hun and in the end, translates into more dead Canadian soldiers. Take it easy on the women and the booze. You are expected to be ready for combat tomorrow if called upon. That is all."

The captain turned and left the mess tent. The sergeants then addressed their squads with essentially the standard message: "Before anyone gets a pass, I want all rifles cleaned and oiled, all of your gas gear cleaned and ready, and all ammunition pouches and field packs loaded. If you hurry, you still might have time to catch the supply trucks returning to Albert."

The squad members scrambled to the tasks and still had time to wash up and get dressed for town. They climbed into the back of the trucks and rode standing up as the trucks jostled and sputtered down the road to Albert. They drove through a shattered countryside of shell craters, ruined houses, and destroyed woods, passing over former trench works now spanned by makeshift bridges. Paul recognized an area of now abandoned trenches where he first took his place at the front.

After an hour of joggling down the road they came to the town of Albert, located just beyond the lines as they were on July 1st. Along the way they passed columns of fresh troops heading for the front and other trucks bearing supplies.

"Maybe they'll start the offensive with green troops," Curtis mused.

"Let them wear down the Hun by the time we get back. Then we can clean up," Dale added.

"Hell of a way to think of those young pups," Paul

said. "They have no idea what they're in for."

"Better them than us," Dale added.

"We'll probably do the fighting," Curtis said. "The greenhorns will be used to collect the dead, just like we once did."

"We don't even know if we are going over the top when we get back," Paul said optimistically.

"We will. That's why they are suddenly giving us some leave. They give a few hours pleasure before sending us out to die," Dale snorted.

"Well, I won't die," Paul said. "I promised that I would return."

"You never know when you time is up," Curtis said. "You can only hope that it will be at the end of a long satisfying life."

"We're going to town for a good time," Dale said. "Let's not talk about dying."

"Yeah," Curtis replied as he lit a cigarette.

Albert was a town adapted to become a soldier's haven. Although lot as large and full of entertainments as Ameins, it still featured bars, brothels and sometimes travelling entertainment troupes. Local vendors were also on hand to try to sell the war-weary troops everything from watches to chocolate. One could purchase with currency, or barter with cigarettes and other hard-to-obtain products from North America.

"I suppose you're going to visit the nearest bordello?" Paul said to Curtis.

"No, I think I'll just go to one of the bars and have a few drinks. I've seen enough of the other to last for a while. How about you?"

"Yeah, the pub sounds fine," Paul replied.

As they climbed from the truck a teenage boy approached them, "Cigarette *monsieur*?" he begged." The lad looked like he hadn't eaten for a day or two.

Curtis pulled a five-franc note from his pocket and said, "Take this instead and buy yourself something to eat."

The lad's face lit up and he replied, *"Merci beaucoup, monsieur, merci."* He turned and ran down the street."

"That was generous," Paul smiled.

"That urchin is too young to smoke anyway. Hopefully he'll buy a loaf of bread or something else to eat."

*   *   *

In the office of the provost marshal, Colonel Wilson and General Cherrington, commander of the Canadian division to which Paul's outfit belonged met to consider the incident concerning Lieutenant Bedford.

"Any Canadian soldiers interviewed deny being witness to how Bedford may have been killed. Since the company was spread over a wide area, it is quite possible that many of them weren't," the provost marshal declared.

"What about the squad to which our suspect was assigned?" Wilson demanded.

"Some of them have already been killed in action and one of his close friends is a PoW," the provost marshal replied.

"What about this Corporal Smith and this Chalmers fellow," Wilson persisted.

"They've all since been promoted," Cherrington scoffed. "Smith is now squad sergeant and Cunningham is his lead corporal. Their captain speaks highly of them and has put them in line for a medal."

"Preposterous," Wilson snorted.

"These Canadians have their own way of doing things, but they are bloody good soldiers," Cherrington said with a note of pride.

"A rather insubordinate bunch I might add," Wilson remarked.

"In reference to your earlier question," the provost marshal said, "Smith and Chalmers will be saved for the court-martial for their questioning."

"If the testimony of the German POW can be taken as true, then the lieutenant was a madman and Cunningham was acting in self-defense." Cherrington stated. Though he was a British officer, he had a great respect for the Canadians he commanded.

"An enlisted man was involved in an altercation with an officer in which the officer was killed, whether it was murder or accident, a serious breach of command has happened and a court-martial will be called." Wilson was adamant.

*   *   *

For the next couple of hours, Paul and Curtis spent time in one of the pubs consuming locally made wine. They both agreed that French wine was better than French beer. Nearly all of the patrons were fellow soldiers. As they talked of old times, Paul said, his voice somewhat slurred, "It's been a long time since we got to sit together in a pub to share a drink or two."

"Yeah, it has been. Too many loose women and girlfriends always seem to get in the way."

"Here's to the loose women and painted ladies," Paul said raising his glass. "To hell with the girlfriends."

"Still bitter about Chelsea, eh?" Curtis asked carefully as he touched Paul's glass with his own.

"She was just a chorus girl anyway," Paul scoffed. "They're a dime, or should I say a *centime,* a dozen. I know, a bob a dozen." Paul laughed heartily and took another swallow of wine.

One of their comrades came into the pub and announced loudly, "Hey, there's a travelling show down the street that features cancan dancers."

"Cancan dancers?" Paul puzzled.

"You know, this French invention where a line of chorus girls flash their bare calves to the beat of lively music."

"Never mind calves, they flash their whole legs," the soldier who came into the bar announced with wide eyes.

"I've heard of them, but I've never actually seen a cancan performance," Paul replied.

"Never seen the cancan?" Curtis said curiously. "I took in a cancan performance when I was on leave in Paris. It's really something."

"Sounds interesting," Paul replied in a nonchalant tone.

"That's what we're gonna do, Rich Kid, we're gonna go see the cancan girls."

"I'll drink to that, Sarge." Then to the soldier who made the announcement, he asked, "When does the show start?"

"In about an hour."

"Lets go early and get a good seat." Curtis said. "To appreciate the cancan girls you need to be in the front row."

Paul, Curtis and several others of their comrades found their way to a large tent that had been set up for the travelling show that had come to entertain the troops. They managed to secure seats in the second row of the rapidly-filling tent.

"Did you see what else was featured?" Paul asked, "There was a crowd between me and the billboard."

"Nothing in particular," Curtis said evenly.

When the show started, the cancan dancers were the first act. A small orchestra sat at one side to provide the lively music for the performance. As the girls whirled around the stage flashing their bared legs to the beat of the music, the hooting and whistling from the soldiers nearly drowned it out.

After the cancan performance, a duet sang K-K-K-Katy and marched around stage as they sang

"K-K-K-Katy, beautiful Katy, you're the only g-g-g-girl that I adore

When the m-m-m-moon shines over the cow shed you be waiting at the k-k-k-kitchen door."

Paul's heart leaped and the influence of alcohol seemed to vanish as the announcer introduced their star performer, "Miss Chelsea Pickford"

"You didn't tell me that Chelsea was performing," Paul complained to Curtis amid the cheering and whistling.

"I didn't know until I saw the billboard."

"You could have warned me."

"I wanted it to be a surprise."

Paul's attention was rapt and he sat under a hypnotic spell as Chelsea sang the soft words of the popular *Soldier Boy*. When the song was in its final verse, Paul stood up and a slow smile crossed Chelsea's face as she noticed him. So entranced was Paul, that he began to walk toward the stage and two bouncers began to move toward him. As the last words faded into wild cheering and whistling from the crowd, Paul sprang up on stage just ahead of the bouncer's grasp into Chelsea's waiting arms.

"Oh, Paul, darling," she moaned with her cheek pressed against his. The cheering was now deafening. "I've missed you so."

"Oh, Chelsea, I love you," Paul gasped in return.

They hugged tightly swaying gently as the manager appeared, shouting, "Bloody hell, throw that blighter off stage."

The bouncers were about to do their duty but several of Paul's comrades from his squad led by Curtis leaped up on stage and stood in the way of the bouncers in threatening confrontation while the crowd cheered on.

"What the blazes is going on?" the manager demanded. "Call the ruddy MP"

"What's the matter with you?" Curtis shouted. "Can't you see, they're in love?"

"I say, darling Paul, we're causing quite a spectacle up here," Chelsea smiled as she looked Paul in the eyes.

"I never noticed," Paul said with a dreamy smile. "I only have eyes and ears for you."

"Oh, Paul darling," Chelsea said kissing him again. "I was a fool to turn down your proposal."

"It is still open you know."

"Then I accept."

"Oh, Chelsea, I love you so."

"This is preposterous," the enraged Chas said. "I have a ruddy show to put on."

"Do you have any more songs?" Paul asked.

"One more."

"Then sing it and we can go for a walk."

Chelsea turned to Chas, still arm in arm with Paul, and said, "Call your goons off, and I'll finish my performance."

"But the bloody soldier has to go."

"Paul stays, if he wishes. Or I'll just bloody well walk away."

"If you walk away, you will be fired and left to find your own way back to England," Chas retorted. "Your singing career will be destroyed."

"She'll sing her song, then we'll take our leave, at least until the next show," Paul said calmly.

"Get your ruddy friends off stage then."

"We'll leave with your bouncers." Curtis said.

Chas motioned for the bouncers to back off; Paul's army buddies did likewise as the crowd chanted, "Chelsea, Chelsea, Chelsea."

The stage cleared save for Paul, who was still holding her hand.

Although her manager was still fuming, Chelsea went ahead with her number with Paul at her side as she sang *Roses Are Blooming in Picardy*. To everyone's surprise Paul duetted the last verse with her, surprising even himself with the quality of his voice.

The song ended with a thunderous round of applause and Chelsea spoke to the audience.

"Thank you all very much, but I must now bid you adieu as I have a date with the soldier who has captured my heart."

There was more wild cheering as both Paul and Chelsea bowed, turned and walked backstage arm in arm.

"I must say you two were a smashing success," Chas confessed. "Too bad you are in the Army, soldier."

"We will take our leave now," Chelsea said. "I don't have another appearance until this evening."

"You *are* coming back I hope?" Chas asked in an urgent tone.

"I will get her back in time," Paul assured him.

When they left the tent, Paul asked cautiously, "Did you say that you actually will marry me?"

"Yes, Paul darling. Ever since I ran out on you that morning, I could think of nothing but you. When the newspapers were full of accounts of heavy fighting in the Somme sector, I feared you might have been killed."

"Not me, I will survive this war and when it is over I

will take you home to Canada," Paul squeezed her waist as they walked along. "Were you surprised when I stood up?"

"Yes, it was like that scene over in London being repeated, except this time I won't let you go."

"What about your singing career? Did you sing before the King?"

"What is a singing career without love? No, I never got to sing in front of the King, but we are supposed to go to Paris early in the new year if I stay with the company."

"Well, I can't promise you that I could take you to Paris, but I can take you to New York. It is not far from Toronto."

"Oh, Paul, that would be marvelous. When are we getting married?"

"As soon as we can. How about when I get a furlough in November? You can plan a proper wedding with your family and I will ask my friend, Curtis, to stand up with me."

"Oh, Paul, that will be so grand."

"Oh, there he is now," Paul said as he saw Cutis and some of the others emerge from the tent. Paul hailed him over and made introductions.

"So this is the lady that has stolen your heart," Curtis smiled. "You have a beautiful voice, Chelsea."

"Thank you. Paul has spoken much about you."

"Rich Kid and I are buds," Curtis laughed as he slapped Paul's back.

"Yes, well would you stand up with me at our wedding, sarge?" Paul asked.

"Your best friend is your sergeant?" Chelsea was surprised.

"We both got promoted a few weeks back. He became my sarge and I am his corporal assistant." Paul grinned as he turned his arm so Chelsea could see his stripes.

"I'd be honoured to stand up with you, Rich Kid. When is the big day?"

"During our next furlough. The wedding will be in Dover, England."

"It's a date. Are you going to invite your sister over to the wedding?"

"I will tell them, but I doubt that any would come because of the U-boat threat."

"I was hoping your family could come over," Chelsea said somewhat downcast.

"Father will be angry, because he will think you to be below my station, and he probably wouldn't let Ginny come because she is only sixteen, even if there weren't any U-boats."

"That is the one problem I will have in marrying you - your family."

"My family will have to learn to accept you, or I will disassociate from them, except for Ginny. She'll accept you without reservation. Frankly I don't care what the others think."

"Well, I'll leave you two to enjoy each other's company," Curtis said, turning to go. "It was a real pleasure to have met you, Chelsea. Paul is a lucky man."

"Oh, Paul darling, it will be such a grand wedding! You can invite as many of your soldier friends as you like. But I am concerned about your family and how they will react. Are you willing to be estranged from your family for me?"

"They will have to accept you, and may I ask, Are you prepared to give up your singing and stage career for me?"

"Absolutely, my darling Paul." They kissed again. "You're sure your sister Ginny will accept me?"

"Positively, my dearest Chelsea," Paul grinned. "You will get along famously, I am sure. I can hardly wait to write and tell her the wedding is back on. Then I shall have to write Mother and tell them about you. Perhaps by the time the war is over, they will be anxious to meet you."

"Oh, Paul darling, you are so optimistic."

Chelsea and Paul spent the remainder of the afternoon walking about in a dreamy state alternating from arm in arm to hand in hand. They tried to choose quiet areas away from the throngs of soldiers, some of whom would beg for Chelsea's autograph, as they made plans for their future together. They even found a small park at the edge of the town where they could sit and talk of their future though the rumble of cannon fire could be heard in the distance. It was agreed that Chelsea would fulfill her commitments to her manager and stay with the entertainment company until the time of the wedding, at which time she would resign.

When Paul suggested that she could still carry on after they were married at least until the war was over, Chelsea hit him with a bombshell.

"Oh, Paul darling, I wouldn't be able to go on for very long, I am in a family way."

"Family way! Like in being pregnant?" his eyes dilated.

"Yes, darling. You must have been planning ahead to make me your wife as conception happened during your furlough that time," Chelsea grinned.

"You are going to have my baby?" Paul was still dumbfounded. "Won't you be disgraced for conceiving a child out of wedlock?"

"Conceiving out of wedlock is forgiven with a wink, as long as the father honours his obligations," Chelsea laughed as she kissed Paul again.

"I will honour them to the last breath in me," Paul replied. "What shall we name our child when it comes?"

"I'll let you pick the names, unless you pick names that I despise, then we'll negotiate," she laughed.

"Let's see... If we have a son we should call him Curtis after my friend. If our child should be a girl we must call her Virginia."

"Virginia is a beautiful name," Chelsea smiled. "And

Curtis is also a fine name. "I'll choose their middle names." Then after a moment she said, "Curtis Paul or Virginia Mae."

"Excellent my darling, a beautiful choice."

Paul brought her back to the tent about a half-hour before the show and the manager was there to greet them.

"So you did come back! Jolly good!" was his comment.

"Of course, Chelsea is a person who honours her commitments," Paul smiled.

"Oh, Chas, Paul and I were talking of our future. I will stay with the company until late November when Paul gets his furlough. Then I will resign and get married. This will give you time to find another singer."

"I suppose there's no stopping you from ending a promising career," Chas sighed.

"I'll be starting a new career as the wife of Paul in Canada when the war is over."

"I suppose I will learn to live with that," Chas replied. "For now, you must get ready for your act."

"Oh, Paul, are you going to stay and watch the show?"

"Yes, definitely. This time I will stay in my seat," he laughed.

They kissed for a long moment before Paul left the backstage area. "I will come to see you before I catch my ride back to the front," Paul promised.

Chapter Twenty

As they rode back to their billets in the back of the truck facing the cold October winds, Paul was silent. He was thinking of how exactly he would compose letters to both his mother and Ginny announcing his planned wedding. He would ask them to come and if they couldn't, would they send Ginny? Neither would probably happen. His father would be furious and go into a rant but he would be utterly powerless to stop the course of true love. Paul managed a chuckle with the thought of his father's rage. He could hardly wait for the later announcement concerning their first grandchild, born of a postmaster's daughter and common entertainer.

By the time they got back, however, it was nearly midnight and Paul was too tired to write. He tried to struggle with a letter to his parents, but the call for 'lights out' came before he got past the first line.

"Looks like you'll have to finish your letters tomorrow night, Rich Kid," Curtis said from his bunk.

"I suppose," Paul sighed, as he folded up his writing pad. "It is something that I feel I should really do tonight."

"No hurry," Dale added. "You said you're gonna survive this war anyway."

"True. I guess I am just excited about marrying Chelsea," Paul replied as he crawled into his bunk. Outside the dull thudding of the cannons blasting away at the German positions could be heard reverberating through the walls of the dugout.

After roll call the following morning, Captain Robbins addressed the entire company.

"After breakfast today, everyone will assemble again in full combat gear. This whole sector of the front is going on the offensive. The objective of the fourth Canadian Division will be to take the key position of Regina Trench. General Haig is confident this time we will break through the enemy lines. The strength of the Hun's forces are down and we have been bombarding him steadily for the last twenty-four hours. The prevailing southwest winds have allowed us to use gas extensively, so the German forces should be very weary. Since we of C Company had a rest in town yesterday, it is deemed that we should lead the charge. One good push should lead to a breakthrough. So put up a good fight and good luck, lads."

"I've heard that line so many times already," Dale said to Paul out of the corner of his mouth."

"What was that, soldier?" the captain barked.

"I was saying, sir, I hope we do break through this time, sir," Dale replied smartly.

"I have every confidence we will," Captain Robbins reiterated. "The Hun has lost twice as many men as we have over the last few months. Their manpower reserves must be running pretty low. So, heads-up lads, lets see what we can do to bring this war to an early end. If Company C can breach the German lines, we'll be the shining star of all the Canadian Army."

Cheers erupted from the men of Company C.

Looking at Curtis who sat near to where the captain was standing, he said quietly, "Do well today and your entire squad will be given medals."

"Yes, sir," Curtis smiled. "We'll do our best, whether or not we are rewarded."

They were sent to breakfast and fed a good ration with a double helping of nearly everything offered.

"Ironic isn't it, that they feed us good before sending us out to get killed," Curtis observed dryly.

"Yeah, we always get extra before going over the top," Paul replied. "It's like giving a condemned man his wish for the last meal before the hanging."

"Who are all these strangers?" Dale asked as he noticed a lot of strange faces in the mess tent.

"Replacements I guess," Paul shrugged.

"Wait a minute," Curtis said. "I recognize two of them that were sent to the stockade for sleeping on duty."

"Oh and there's one called Tom Smuthers," he was in for being a few days AWOL."

"They're on punishment duty," Curtis noted. "Soldiers on punishment always go in the first wave attack." His voice trailed off as he added, "So are we."

"What did we do?" Dale wondered.

"It's me. What I did," Paul blurted.

"Now don't go judging yourself," Curtis said, although the thought also occurred to him.

After breakfast the company was marshalled outside. Each sergeant inspected his squad to assure his combat gear, especially his respirator, was in order as squad members stood at rigid attention. With all in order and reported to their superiors, the company chaplain then addressed the assembled soldiers.

With rifles at their sides and helmets removed and bowed heads, they recited the Lord's Prayer, then listened to the chaplain pray for strength for victory over the 'terrible Hun.' As Paul listened, the pastor's voice seemed far away. He was calling on God to give them strength to kill their fellow man, indeed fellow Christians. Paul could not help but wonder if, on the other side of no-man's-land, another chaplain was also calling on God in German to give *their* troops strength for victory. Truly it must pain God very much to see his children killing each other in His name. It was indeed, a strange and mad world that Paul had found himself to be in. As the chaplain closed his sermon with, "Jesus Christ our Lord, Amen," Paul wondered how one would say that phrase in German.

When the service was over, the captain spoke. "At ease, men." The soldiers relaxed their rigid stance and he continued, "Again I wish you luck and success today, queue up for your grog and your squad leaders will take you to your places at the front trenches. Dismissed."

The soldiers, even the tea-totallers, took their grog, consisting of a mug of powerful rum. It was strong enough to dull their senses, but not so strong as to impair their ability on the battlefield. The cannons were still blasting away at the German positions drawing the occasional return fire from still functioning German artillery, as they filed into the front row of trenches. Despite the glow Paul felt from the grog, he clutched his rifle with cold, clammy hands as he knew the Grim Reaper lay in wait on the other side of no-man's-land.

*   *   *

Meanwhile at regimental headquarters, Lieutenant Colonel Jamison sat behind his desk in contemplation. All four companies of his battalion were going into battle this morning. He recalled the conversation with his regimental commander the previous day that his battalion would lead the charge. He could choose which company would conduct the first wave, generally considered a suicide mission. The stockade had been emptied of undesirables and trouble-makers to fill the gaps in the company manpower depleted from previous engagements for this first wave as per custom. He then had to agonize over which company to select .

All four company CO's were informed at a battalion level situation meeting that any one of the companies could be chosen as he hadn't made up his mind and might have to draw straws. As the meeting drew to a close, a courier arrived with a note. They observed that Jamison's face dropped and he went into deep thought for a moment. Finally he said, "Company C will conduct the first wave assault. The meeting is over but Captain Robbins, you and your lieutenants please remain."

When the others had left he explained. "Your company has been selected for this first wave, for a few very important reasons. One is, it is the most manpower-depleted of all my companies and thus we'll give you all the dregs from the stockade to fill the gaps."

"Understandable sir, but I was hoping to be spared as both Sergeant Smith and Corporal Cunningham are in my company. I was hoping they would be spared first wave. I do have them in for special citation for battlefield valour."

"Yes, I'm aware of their record and it is a painful decision that I should send them on the first wave, but read this." Jamison handed Robbins the note delivered to him.

Captain Robbins read the essence of the note aloud in a small voice, "The MP will arrive tomorrow morning to arrest Corporal Paul Cunningham on charges of being responsible for the death of Lieutenant Bedford. Do not grant him any leave. They will also carry subpoenas for Sergeant Smith and Lance Corporal Chalmers to appear at his court-martial. Oh My God!"

"You know what this means?" Jamison said gravely.

"They'll shoot Cunningham."

"Or at very least give him a sentence of time at hard labour. Smith could be dragged into this also and end up losing his stripes."

"So that is why you selected my company."

"Better to let them die like men in battle, than in disgrace."

"But, they'll be expecting to arrest Cunningham," Robbins said. "Won't it come back on you if he is sent into battle instead?"

"Military justice is swift and brutal," Jamison said. "They want Cunningham's head, whether it is lost on the battlefield or at the wall doesn't matter. If he dies in battle, at least his family can be informed that he died honourably in the course of duty. In light of his record, both he and his family deserve that much."

"And if he dies in battle and Smith lives?"

"In all likelihood the matter will be quickly dropped, though they still might take a statement from Smith for the record."

"He still won't be indicted?"

"Probably not," Jamison shrugged. "This is all in confidence until after the attack and or arrest, gentlemen."

"Yes, sir," They responded almost in unison.

Although Jamison had spoken bravely to his subordinate officers the previous day, he could still get his fingers slapped for sending Corporal Cunningham into battle rather than holding him back for the arrest.

There was a knock on the door and a trio of military police led by a Major Williams arrived at the colonel's office. They entered upon his call and saluted their superior officer as Jamison rose from his chair. The major stepped forward to address the colonel while the other two remained in the background.

Upon being admitted, the major said as he saluted, "Colonel Jamison of the North Ontario regiment, I presume, sir."

"Quite correct, Major," the colonel replied as he answered the major's salute. "To what do I owe the honour of a visit by the MP?" though he knew quite well why they were there. Then with a laugh added, "Am I under arrest?"

"No, but one of your men is."

"Oh, have one of my boys been causing trouble in town?" Jamison laughed feigning ignorance.

"Not that, sir," the major replied seriously. "I believe you have a Corporal Paul Cunningham in your regiment, in Company C."

"Quite correct," Colonel Jamison replied. "He doesn't seem like the troublesome kind though. A few weeks back when I promoted him to full corporal, I checked his record and it was perfectly clean. What's up?"

"It seems," Major Williams replied carefully, "that Corporal Cunningham while in the temporary service of the South London battalion, appeared to have had an altercation with his commander, Lieutenant Bedford. Bedford was killed ."

"Oh my God, this is serious," Jamison replied, still playing the charade, "but why did it take you so long to react? It's been over a month since B & C companies were returned to the corps."

"The squad leader reported the lieutenant as killed by enemy fire. However, further investigation, at the insistence of his family, revealed that the bullet wound in his head was not from a German Mauser, but his own pistol at close range. Any soldiers in that area we sought out for questioning are either dead, like the then sergeant, or denied knowledge of witnessing the exact moment the lieutenant was killed. The most we could get out of anyone was that they were having a fierce argument over a German prisoner. Captain Walker, their company commander at the time, said that Lieutenant Bedford was very unpopular." Then with brief pause the major continued, " I will have a subpoena for his close comrades, Sergeant Smith and Corporal Dale

Chalmers to appear as witnesses at the court-martial"

"I see. It seems incredible that a quiet unassuming soldier like Cunningham would murder an officer."

"Lieutenant Bedford's death could have been an accident, sir, but there was an altercation between an officer and an enlisted man, resulting in the officer's death. Our suspect will have to answer before a court-martial," the major said gravely. "There is already evidence of mutiny in the French and Russian armies; the British Army dare not show any breach of rank"

"Well, all four companies of my regiment are going into battle this morning." The colonel glanced at his watch and continued, "Any moment now Company C to which Cunningham belongs, will be going over the top."

"We were expecting to make an arrest and escort a prisoner to the stockade," the major said tersely.

"Then we shall have to wait until the attack is over, assuming any of them survive."

"This is most improper," the major grumbled. "We came for a prisoner and all we'll likely get is a corpse."

"I was not instructed to hold Cunningham back," Jamison said blandly, "just not to give him any leave. All the troublemakers are going over the top on the first wave."

"How long sir, will it take before we know if Cunningham survived?" the major grumbled

"It will probably take several hours, or maybe even days to determine how the battle unfolds and before roll calls determine who survived. If he is killed or wounded straight off, your wait won't be too long."

"I hope not sir, or we'll have to inform the provost marshal."

"I'll contact Captain Robbins to keep as close an eye on Cunningham's fate as possible.

*   *   *

Meanwhile at the front trenches the cry went out, "Fix your bayonets!" There was a clatter as the soldiers secured their bayonets to the ends of their rifles.

Then the cannons laid a barrage along the front German trenches. The whistle blew, followed by the cry, "Over the top lads."

Instinctively, Paul, Curtis and the others scrambled up the pallets and leapt over the barbed wire into no-man's-land. They fanned out and charged headlong toward the enemy lines.

The continuing artillery barrage kept the Germans off balance, and they were able to breach the first line of trenches. Most of the German soldiers had retreated to their second line of trenches with very little fighting, Then, as the men of Curtis' squad stopped to catch their breaths, the Germans opened up with trench mortars. Some of their shells contained chlorine. As the deadly greenish cloud began to fill the front trenches, an overpowering odour of bleach permeated the air. Curtis and Paul scrambled upon the rear parapet to get away from the gas long enough to get their respirators on. As they did so, Paul cried, "Look out, Curtis, a sniper!"

He sprang to knock his friend down as the German sniper fired. "I think they got me," Paul winced as he rolled off of Curtis. "I feel a sharp pain in my side."

They rolled into a shallow shell crater safe from both the sniper's bullets and the chlorine filled trench, while a constant exchange of gunfire and artillery shells passed over their heads.

"You've been hit in the side, buddy," Curtis said gravely as he saw blood trickling from two places in the side of his tunic. "Let me fix you up."

"No! Go on," Paul gasped. "You're supposed to lead

the charge and let the stretcher-bearers find me."

"Not before I help you stop the bleeding," Curtis insisted. "You saved my life, Rich Kid. I owe it to you. Now let me help you."

"Too late," Paul coughed as he pulled his respirator off. Blood was trickling out of his mouth. "I can feel. . . the life blood. . . draining. . . out of me."

Paul shifted one of his legs and both he and Curtis noticed that the puttee was coming unwound.

"You never could tie your puttees properly," Curtis laughed weakly as he also removed his respirator.

"Yeah. . . You. . . were the best friend. . . a rich kid. . . could have," Paul gasped. "You can have. . . my extra socks. . . Share my cigarettes. . . and candy. . . with the others."

"What is this 'were'?" Curtis said with a brave face. "You are going to survive this war, remember? I'm gonna be best man at your wedding."

"I guess I broke my promise. . . to Chelsea. . . and my sister. . . Forgive me. . . Ginny," Paul gasped as he was growing drowsy. "Promise me, Curtis. . . my friend."

"Yes. Go on," Curtis choked.

"Promise to. . . to write to Chelsea. Her address. . . is in my kit. . . the army doesn't know she is my fiancee. . . They won't tell her. Tell her. . . tell her I'll love her through all eternity. . . And. . . Keep on singing. The angels up there. . . will remind me. . . of her. . . voice."

"I promise, but there'll be no need. You're gonna live."

"Tell her. . . tell her to name our child. . . the names we agreed to. . . especially if it is a son."

"Chelsea is pregnant with your son, Rich Kid?" Curtis grinned broadly.

"Yeah," Paul grinned weakly. "That time on leave."

"Then you gotta live, to see your son."

"Fall back," came the order as a line of artillery fire allowed the company to retreat. Curtis flung Paul over his shoulder as they went back to the Canadian lines. He called for the stretcher-bearers and laid Paul down on the fire-step saying, "We're safe now, buddy, we failed again to breach the Hun." Paul was very still and his eyes were wide and unseeing.

It was a week later before Chelsea caught up with her mail and read the words, sobbing as her tears fell upon the paper.

Dear Chelsea,
It is with heavy heart that I write to tell you that Paul fell in battle this morning. He put up a good fight and died bravely. I find this letter very hard to write as Paul was not only my best friend, but he saved my life as the bullets he caught were meant for me. He saw the sniper and pushed me down. In his final words all he could think of was you, for he said, 'Tell Chelsea I will love her for all eternity. Tell Chelsea to keep on singing.' He said the angels will remind him of your voice. Also he said to be sure to name his son the name you agreed upon.
Kindest Regards
Curtis

Back in Toronto, a red-eyed Robert, held his sobbing wife Claire while his hand, that was still clutching that terrible black edged telegram, was still trembling. All his hopes and dreams for his son were gone and he wondered how he would ever be able to tell Ginny.

After Note

Under pressure from his junior officers who grew tired of the appalling waste of manpower in a futile battle that was going nowhere, General Haig finally called off the Battle of the Somme in November of 1916. That terrible slaughter, which had begun on July 1st of that year, claimed over a million battlefield casualties without either victory or significant territorial gain for the armies of the British Empire. Of this butchery, the Canadian Army had sustained over twenty-four thousand casualties.

About the Author

Eric John Brown was born on August 13, 1947 the youngest son of John and Ruby Brown. He was raised on a farm in the community of Magnolia about one hundred kilometres west of Edmonton, Alberta.

Magnolia was, during his childhood, a hamlet consisting of a store, a church and a community hall. The community was a closely-knit one and his family was a warm loving one. During his early grades, he attended a one-roomed school about a mile from home then completed his remaining grades at Seba Beach School from which he graduated. He has always been a keen student of modern history, geography, and science.

Virtually all of his working life has been spent first with Canadian National Railways Signals Department and later with TransAlta at the local Sundance power generating plant.

While on a trip to Scotland to visit relatives in 1971 he met his future wife, Isabella. They were married in Scotland nearly two years later and have since raised two sons, John and Colin.

The author began writing stories when he was thirteen years old but most of his early writings were of the science-fiction genre. Later, as he became more skilled at character development, he turned to standard fiction. He has also developed a keen interest in the ethnic and linguistic background of the vast mosaic of peoples that make up Canada. He, in particular, has focused on peoples seldom mentioned in mainstream literature such as Finns, Latvians, Ukrainians and Scandinavians.

The saga of *Ginny*, his first publication, was conceived when he was only twenty-three years old. At the time however, he lacked the necessary writing skills to tackle a work of this magnitude. It remained, however, in the back of his mind like bedrock, even as he worked on other writings. The details of *Ginny* slowly filled in over the years. Finally after the acquisition of a home computer in 1994, the author tackled this long overdue novel in earnest. As the author set to writing, what was originally to be the story of a community, a strange thing happened. In the author's own words, "the character, Ginny, leaped out of my imagination and took control of the saga making it her story." Since that time this powerful and warm, loving character has captured the hearts of hundreds of readers of all ages.

The result of his literary labours was the publication of *Ginny* on December 11, 1998. From the first day of publication *Ginny* has been well received by readers, reviewers, bookstores, libraries and the general media. With the highly successful publication of *Ginny* via the route of self-publishing, the author has continued to write novels which have found broad appeal on the marketplace.

Ginny
A Canadian Story of Love & Friendship

Ginny is a rich girl from Toronto who dares, against her family's wishes, to elope with Danish immigrant named Marty Polsen to his homestead in Alberta. Ginny faces many challenges on the homestead such as learning how to cook, coping with homesickness, being chased by a bear, and a difficult childbirth that nearly kills her. With the support of both her loving husband Marty, and her dear friends, Ingrid and Gina, Ginny perseveres.

As you trace Ginny's life, from a time when she was a rich girl adjusting to the rigours of the homestead, to a time when she is offering wise counsel to her grandchildren of the baby boomer era - you will come to appreciate that this work is a triumphant story of love and friendship.

Ingrid

AN IMMIGRANT'S TALE

Ingrid is only fourteen years old when she is torn away from all that is familiar including her dear friend, Sigrud. This, because her father had chosen to immigrate from Sweden to Canada in 1910 with his family. Ingrid is frightened at the prospect of having to learn a new language, coming to a strange new frontier land and she pines for her friend left behind. When settled in her new home, Ingrid, is pursued by two undesirable suitors, one is a shy clumsy man and the other a raucous ruffian. When Ingrid finally meets and marries the love of her life all seems well, but tragedy and disappointment still stalk her.

Much of this story takes place with World War I looming in the background and the Great War has its effect on both Ingrid and her neighbours.

Anna
An Odyssey to Freedom

Anna is a bright eighteen-year-old girl, a member of a happy family and has a bright future ahead of her. Then her world is shattered when the Soviet Union forcibly annexes her tiny homeland of Latvia in the summer of 1940. A year later it is conquered again, by the Nazis. Anna's family is destroyed and she is forced to live by her wits. Her only hope is to somehow find her brother, who is abroad, and the young man in her life who is also lost in these brutal crosscurrents of history. Her only dream is to reach the faraway golden land of Canada. Thus, begins Anna's incredible odyssey to freedom.

To the Last Tree Standing

Following up an article in an outdoors magazine, Freelance writer Jill Tompkins sets out to find a mysterious mountain man simply known as Brother Nature or commonly Bro. He is the self-appointed protector of a beautiful stretch of forest in Montana. As she begins her trek into the forest, Jill discovers that there is more mystery here than she bargained for. She is followed by a hit man employed by a ruthless logging magnate, whose mission is to kill Bro and she is watched over by a sympathetic forest ranger. As she plunges deeper into the forest after the elusive Bro, the plot thickens, the mystery grows, and the suspense builds.

Bro is a fast-moving tale of conservation, ecology, and defense of the innocent. It is a must read for all who fight to save our environment from those who would pillage and destroy our precious natural heritage.

Third Time Lucky

Jane Brody was "as plain as dirt and tough as nails", so her mail-order suitor Ethan Phillips had declared. He also declared that she was "one hell of a cook and could sing like a lark" especially when she sang that haunting ballad *Never-ending Road*. Their many, often humorous confrontations in which her prim frumpish ways clash with his crude sardonic manner, threaten to destroy their precarious relationship at any given moment.

When Jane, the perennial wallflower, becomes entangled in a love triangle with Ethan and the lovable Irish moonshiner, Sean O'Malley, Ethan is at a loss how to cope, and is left to ponder his belief than either bad luck runs in threes or that the third time can also be lucky.

For additional copies of

Anna – Her odyssey to Freedom

Ginny - A Canadian Story of Love and
Friendship

Ingrid – An Immigrant's Tale

The Promise

To The Last Tree Standing

Third Time Lucky

Write to
Magnolia Press
General Delivery
Entwistle, Alberta
T0E 0S0

Or

E-Mail mag_press@hotmail.com